C000156131

AIRPORT
SPOTTING GUIDES

Europe

MATT FALCUS

Second Edition 2012

Cover design by Wright Angle Design

ISBN 978-0-9567187-2-3

British Library Cataloguing-in-Publication Data

A catalogue record for this book is available from the British Library.

Published by Destinworld Publishing Ltd.

www.destinworld.com

All photographs © Matthew Falcus

Contents

Airports in Sweden

Airports in Switzerland

Airports in Turkey

Airports in Ukraine

Airports in United Kingdom and Republic of Ireland

This page has been intentionally left blank.

Introduction

Since the first edition of this book came out in 2008, there have been a number of changes at many of Europe's airports. New runways have been built at Amsterdam, Frankfurt and Malaga (although plans to open new ones in the UK have controversially been scrapped). Many airlines have also come and gone, changing the experience of visiting many airports for the enthusiast. In 2012 we'll also see the new airport of Berlin Brandenburg open, as the older facilities close.

We've also seen a vast reduction in the number of classic Russian (and even Western) aircraft types in European skies, leaving many to turn to storage airports and museums to catch up with these now historic aircraft.

This new edition includes a complete update of the airports covered previously, including fresh insights into the places to watch aircraft, the airlines serving the airport, and facilities such as hotels and nearby aviation attractions. The book also sees the addition of many new European airports' details, which will hopefully enable you to plan spotting trips further afield to some very interesting places.

To read regular updates, news articles and trip reports from airports around Europe and further afield, visit the Airport Spotting Blog at www.airportspotting. com, which is run by the author.

Other books by the author:

▶ Airport Spotting Guides USA (ISBN 978-0-9559281-8-5)

▶ Airport Spotting Guides Far East & Australasia (ISBN 978-0-9567187-1-6)

▶ Last Chance to Fly (ISBN 978-0-9567187-0-9)

This page has been intentionally left blank.

Commercial Airports by Country

This list gives details of the principal commercial airports in each country of Europe where you can expect to find regular airline and/or cargo flights.

ALBANIA
Tirana International Airport LATI/TIA

ANDORRA
No Fixed Wing Airports

ARMENIA
Gymuri Shirak International Airport UDSG/LWN

Yerevan Zvartnots International Airport UDYZ/EVN

AUSTRIA
Graz Airport LOWG/GRZ

Innsbruck Airport LOWI/INN

Klagenfurt Airport LOWK/KLU

Linz Blue Danube Airport LOWL/LNZ

Salzburg W. A. Mozart Airport LOWS/SZG

Vienna Schwechat International Airport LOWW/VIE

AZERBAIJAN
Baku Heydar Aliyev International Airport UBBB/GYD

Ganja Airport UBBG/KVD

Lenkoran International Airport UB10

Nakhchivan Airport UBBN/NAJ

BELARUS
Minsk-1 Airport UMMM/MHP

Minsk International Airport (Minsk-2) UMMS/MSQ

BELGIUM
Antwerp International Airport EBAW/ANR

Brussels Zaventem Airport EBBR/BRU

Charleroi-Brussels South Airport EBCI/CRL

Kortrijk-Wevelgem International Airport EBKT/KJK

Liege Airport EBLG/LGG

Ostend-Bruges International Airport EBOS/OST

BOSNIA AND HERZEGOVINA
Banja Luka International Airport LQBK/BNX

Sarajevo International Airport LQSA/SJJ

Tuzla International Airport LQTZ/TZL

BULGARIA
Bourgas Airport LBBG/BOJ

Plovdiv Airport LBPD/PDV

Sofia Airport LBSF/SOF

Varna Airport LBWN/VAR

CROATIA
Bol Airport LDSB/BWK

Dubrovnik Airport LDDU/DBV

Osijek Airport LDOS/OSI

Pula Airport LDPL/PUY

Rijeka Airport LDRI/RJK

Split Airport LDSP/SPU

Zadar Airport LDZD/ZAD

Zagreb Airport LDZA/ZAG

CYPRUS
Ercan International Airport LCEN/ECN

Larnaca International Airport LCLK/LCA

Paphos International Airport LCPH/PFO

RAF Akrotiri LCRA/AKT

CZECH REPUBLIC
Brno-Tuřany Airport LKTB/BRQ

Karlovy Vary Airport LKKV/KLV

Ostrava Leos Janacek Airport LKMT/OSR

Prague Ruzyne Airport LKPR/PRG

Kunovice Airport LKKU/UHE

DENMARK
Aalborg Airport EKYT/AAL
Aarhus Airport EKAH/AAR
Billund Airport EKBI/BLL
Bornholm Airport EKRN/RNN
Copenhagen Kastrup Airport EKCH/CPH
Copenhagen Roskilde Airport EKRK/RKE
Esbjerg Airport EKEB/EBJ
Karup Airport EKKA/KRP
Læsø Airport EKLS/BYR
Odense Airport EKOD/ODE
Sønderborg Airport EKSB/SGD

ESTONIA
Kärdla Airport EEKA/KDL
Kuressaare Airport EEKE/URE
Pärnu Airport EEPU/EPU
Tallinn Lennart Meri Airport EETN/TLL
Tartu Airport EETU/TAY

FINLAND
Helsinki Vantaa Airport EFHK/HEL
Ivalo Airport EFIV/IVL
Joensuu Airport EFJO/JOE
Jyväskylä Airport EFJY/JYV
Kajaani Airport EFKI/KAJ
Kemi-Tornio Airport EFKE/KEM
Kittilä Airport EFKT/KTT
Kuopio Airport EFKU/KUO
Kussamo Airport EFKS/KAO
Lappeenranta Airport EFLP/LPP
Mariehamm Airport EFMA/MHQ
Oulu Airport EFOU/OUL
Rovaniemi Airport EFRO/RVN
Seinäjoki Airport EFSI/SJY
Tampere-Pirkkala Airport EFTP/TMP
Vaasa Airport EFVA/VAA
Varkaus Airport EFVR/VRK

FRANCE

Ajaccio Airport LFKJ/AJA

Angers Loire Airport LFJR/ANE

Annecy Haute-Savoie Airport LFLP/NCY

Aurillac Airport LFLW/AUR

Avignon Airport LFMV/AVN

Basel-Mulhouse-Freiburg EuroAirport LFSB/MLH

Bastia Poretta Airport LFKB/BIA

Beauvais Tille Airport LFOB/BVA

Bergerac Dordogne Périgord Airport LFBE/EGC

Béziers Cap d'Agde Airport LFMU/BZR

Biarritz-Anglet-Bayonne Airport LFBZ/BIQ

Bordeaux – Mérignac Airport LFBD/BOD

Brest Bretagne Airport LFRB/BES

Brive Souillac Airport LFSL/BVE

Caen Carpiquet Airport LFRK/CFR

Calvi Sainte-Catherine Airport LFKC/CLY

Carcassonne Salvaza Airport LFMK/CCF

Castres – Mazamet Airport LFCK/DCM

Chambéry Airport LFLB/CMF

Châteauroux-Centre "Marcel Dassault" Airport LFLX/CHR

Cherbourg Airport LFRC/CER

Clermont-Ferrand Auvergne Airport LFLC/CFE

Dijon Bourgogne Airport LFSD/DIJ

Dinard-Saint Malo Airport LFRD/DNR

Figari Sud-Corse Airport LFKF/FSC

Grenoble Airport LFLS/GNB

La Rochelle Airport LFBH/LRH

Lannion Cote de Granit Airport LFRO/LAI

Le Havre Airport LFOH/LEH

Le Touquet Airport LFAT/LTQ

Lille Airport LFQQ/LIL

Limoges Bellegarde Airport LFBL/LIG

Lorient South Brittany Airport LFRH/LRT

Lourdes Le Puy Airport LFHP/LPY

Lyon-Saint Exupéry Airport LFLL/LYS

Marseille Provence Airport LFML/MRS
Metz-Nancy-Lorraine Airport LFJL/ETZ
Montpellier Airport LFMT/MPL
Nantes Atlantique Airport LFRS/NTE
Nice Côte d'Azur Airport LFMN/NCE
Nîmes-Alès-Camargue-Cévennes Airport LFTW/FNI
Paris – Charles de Gaulle Airport LFPG/CDG
Paris – Le Bourget Airport LFPB/LBG
Paris – Orly Airport LFPO/ORY
Pau Pyrenees Airport LFBP/PUF
Perpignan Airport LFMP/PGF
Poitiers Airport LFBI/PIS
Quimper Cornouaille Airport LFRQ/UIP
Rennes Saint-Jacques Airport LFRN/RNS
Rodez Marcillac Airport LFCR/RDZ
Rouen Airport LFOP/URO
Saint-Brieuc Armor Airport LFRT/SBK
Saint-Étienne Bouthéon Airport LFMH/EBU
Strasbourg Airport LFST/SXB
Tarbes-Lourdes-Pyrenees Airport LFBT/LDE
Toulon-Hyères Airport LFTH/TLN
Toulouse Blagnac Airport LFBO/TLS
Tours Val de Loire Airport LFOT/TUF
Troyes Barberey Airport LFQB/QYR

GEORGIA
Batumi International Airport UGSB/BUS
Kopitnari Airport UGKO/KUT
Tbilisi International Airport UGTB/TBS

GERMANY
Augsburg Airport EDMA/AGB
Baden-Baden/Karlsruhe Airpark EDSB/FKB
Berlin Schönefeld Airport (to become Berlin Brandenburg Airport) EDDB/SXF
Berlin Tegel Airport (closing June 2012) EDDT/TXL
Bremen Airport EDDW/BRE
Bremerhaven Airport EDWB/BRV

Cologne Bonn Airport EDDK/CGN

Dortmund Airport EDLW/DTM

Dresden Airport EDDC/DRS

Düsseldorf International Airport EDDL/DUS

Emden Airport EDWE/EME

Erfurt Airport EDDE/ERF

Frankfurt/Rhein-Main Airport EDDF/FRA

Frankfurt-Hahn Airport EDFH/HHN

Friedrichshafen Airport EDNY/FDH

Hamburg Airport EDDH/HAM

Hamburg Finkenwerder Airport EDHI/XFW

Hannover-Langenhagen Airport EDDV/HAJ

Heligoland Airport EDXH/HGL

Heringsdorf Airport EDAH/HDF

Hof-Plauen Airport EDQM/HOQ

Kiel Airport EDHK/KEL

Leipzig/Halle Airport EDDP/LEJ

Lübeck Airport EDHL/LBC

Magdeburg-Cochstedt Airport EDBC/CSO

Memmingen Airport EDJA/FMM

Munich Airport EDDM/MUC

Münster Osnabrück Airport EDDG/FMO

Nuremberg Airport EDDN/NUE

Paderborn Lippstadt Airport EDLP/PAD

Rostock-Laage Airport ETNL/RLG

Saarbrücken Airport EDDR/SCN

Stuttgart Airport EDDS/STR

Weeze (Niederrhein) Airport EDLV/NRN

Sylt Airport EDXW/GWT

Zweibrücken Airport EDRZ/ZQW

GREECE

Aktion National Airport LGPZ/PVK

Alexandroupolis International Airport LGAL/AXD

Athens Eleftherios Venizelos International Airport LGAV/ATH

Chania International Airport LGSA/CHQ

Chios Island National Airport LGHI/JKH

Corfu International Airport LGKR/CFU
Heraklion International Airport LGIR/HER
Kalamata International Airport LGKL/KLX
Karpathos Island National Airport LGKY/JKL
Kavala International Airport LGKV/KVA
Kefalonia Island International Airport LGKF/EFL
Kos Island International Airport LGKO/KGS
Lemnos International Airport LGLM/LXS
Mykonos Island National Airport LGMK/JMK
Mytilene International Airport LGMT/MJT
Nea Anchialos National Airport (Volos) LGBL/VOL
Rhodes International Airport LGRP/RHO
Samos International Airport LGSM/SMI
Santorini (Thira) National Airport LGSR/JTR
Skiathos Island National Airport LGSK/JSI
Thessaloniki International Airport LGTS/SKG
Zakynthos International Airport LGZA/ZTH

HUNGARY
Budapest Liszt Ferenc International Airport LHBP/BUD
Debrecen International Airport LHDC/DEB
Sármellék International (Fly Balaton) Airport LHSM/SOB

ICELAND
Akureyri Airport BIAR/AEY
Egilsstaðir Airport BIEG/EGS
Ísafjörður Airport BIIS/IFJ
Keflavik International Airport BIKF/KEF
Reykjavik Airport BIRK/RKV

IRELAND
Cork Airport EICK/ORK
Donegal Airport EIDL/CFN
Dublin Airport EIDW/DUB
Galway Airport EICM/GWY
Ireland West Airport Knock EIKN/NOC
Kerry Airport EIKY/KIR
Shannon Airport EINN/SNN
Waterford Airport EIWF/WAT

ITALY

Alghero-Fertila Airport LIEA/AHO

Ancona-Falconara Airport LIPY/AOI

Bari-Palese Airport LIBD/BRI

Bergamo Orio al Serio Airport LIME/BGY

Bologna-Borgo Panigale Airport LIPE/BLQ

Bolzano-Dolomiti Airport LIPB/BZO

Brescia-Montichiari Airport LIPO/VBS

Brindisi-Casale Airport LIBR/BDS

Cagliari-Elmas Airport LIEE/CAG

Catania-Fontanarossa Airport LICC/CTA

Crotone Airport LIBC/CRV

Cuneo-Levaldigi Airport LIMZ/CUF

Elba Marina di Campo Airport LIRJ/EBA

Florence-Peretola Airport LIRQ/FLR

Foggia Airport LIBF/FOG

Forli Airport LIPK/FRL

Genoa Airport LIMJ/GOA

Lamezia Terme Airport LICA/SUF

Lampedusa Airport LICD/LMP

Milan-Linate Airport LIML/LIN

Milan-Malpensa Airport LIMC/MXP

Naples-Capodichino Airport LIRN/NAP

Olbia – Costa Smeralda Airport LIEO/OLB

Palermo-Punta Raisi Airport LICJ/PMO

Pantelleria Airport LICG/PNL

Parma Airport LIMP/PMF

Perugia-Sant'Egidio Airport LIRZ/PEG

Pescara Abruzzo Airport LIBP/PSR

Pisa-San Giusto Airport LIRP/PSA

Reggio Calabria Airport LICR/REG

Rimini-Miramare Airport LIPR/RMI

Rome-Ciampino Airport LIRA/CIA

Rome-Fiumicini Leonardo da Vinci Airport LIRF/FCO

Tortoli-Arbatax Airport LIET/TTB

Trapani-Birgi Airport LICT/TPS

Treviso-Sant'Angelo Airport LIPH/TSF
Trieste Friuli-Venezia Giulia Airport LIPQ/TRS
Turin-Caselle Airport LIMF/TRN
Venice Marco Polo Airport LIPZ/VCE
Verona-Villafranca Airport LIPX/VRN

KAZAKHSTAN
Almaty International Airport UAAA/ALA
Aktau Airport UATE/SCO
Aktobe Airport UATT/AKX
Astana International Airport UACC/TSE
Karaganda Sary-Arka Airport UAKK/KGF
Kostanay Airport UAUU/KSN
Oral Ak Zhol Airport UARR/URA
Oskemen Airport UASK/UKK
Pavlodar Airport UASP/PWQ
Kyzylorda Airport UAOO/KZO
Semey Airport UASS/PLX
Shymkent Airport UAII/CIT

LATVIA
Daugavpils International Airport EVDA/DGP (due to open 2013)
Liepāja International Airport EVLA/LPX
Riga International Airport EVRA/RIX

LIECHTENSTEIN
No Fixed Wing Airports

LITHUANIA
Kaunas International Airport EYKA/KUN
Palanga International Airport EYPA/PLQ
Vilnius International Airport EYVI/VNO

LUXEMBOURG
Luxembourg Findel Airport ELLX/LUX

MACEDONIA
Ohrid St Paul the Apostle Airport LWOH/OHD
Skopje Alexander the Great Airport LWSK/SKP

MALTA
Malta Luqa International Airport LMML/MLA

MOLDOVA
Chişinău International Airport LUKK/KIV

MONACO
No Fixed Wing Airports

MONTENEGRO
Podgorica Airport LYPG/TGD

Tivat Airport LYTV/TIV

NETHERLANDS
Amsterdam Schiphol Airport EHAM/AMS

Eindhoven Airport EHEH/EIN

Groningen Airport Eelde EHGG/GRQ

Maastricht Aachen Airport EHBK/MST

Rotterdam The Hague Airport EHRD/RTM

Woensdrecht Air Base EHWO/WOE

NORWAY
Ålesund Airport ENAL/AES

Alta Airport ENAT/ALF

Bardufoss Airport ENDU/BDU

Bergen Airport ENBR/BGO

Bodø Airport ENBO/BOO

Harstad/Narvik Airport, ENEV/EVE

Haugesund Airport ENHD/HAU

Kirkenes Airport ENKR/KKN

Kristiansand Airport ENCN/KRS

Kristiansund Airport ENKB/KSU

Molde Airport ENML/MOL

Oslo Gardermoen ENGM/OSL

Oslo Rygge Moss Airport ENRY/RYG

Sandefjord Airport Torp ENTO/TRF

Stavanger Airport ENZV/SVG

Svalbard Airport ENSB/LYR

Tromsø Airport ENTC/TOS
Trondheim Airport ENVA/TRD

POLAND
Bydgoszcz Ignacy Jan Pederewski Airport EPBY/BZG
Gdańsk Lech Wałęsa Airport EGPD/GDN
Krakow John Paul II International Airport EPKK/KRK
Katowice International Airport EPKT/KTW
Łódź Władysław Reymont Airport EPLL/LCJ
Poznań Ławica Airport EPPO/POZ
Rzeszów-Jasionka Airport EPRZ/RZE
Szczytno-Szymany International Airport EPSY/SZY
Szczecin-Goleniów "Solidarność" Airport EPSC/SZZ
Warsaw Frederic Chopin Airport EPWA/WAW
Wroclaw Copernicus Airport EPWR/WRO
Zielona Gora Airport EPZG/IEG

PORTUGAL
Faro Airport LPFR/FAO
Lisbon Portela Airport LPPT/LIS
Porto Francisco Sa Carneiro Airport LPPR/OPO

ROMANIA
Arad International Airport LRAR/ARW
Bacău International Airport LRBC/BCM
Bucharest Băneasa International Airport LRBS/BBU
Bucharest Otopeni International Airport LROP/OTP
Cluj-Napoca International Airport LRCL/CLJ
Constanta International Airport LRCK/CND
Craiova Airport LRCV/CRA
Iași International Airport LRIA/IAS
Oradea International Airport LROD/OMR
Satu Mare International Airport LRSM/SUJ
Sibiu International Airport LRSB/SBZ
Târgu Mureș International Airport LRTM/TSR
Traian Vuia International Airport LRTR/TCE

SAN MARINO
No Fixed Wing Airports

SERBIA
Belgrade Nikola Tesla International Airport LYBE/BEG
Pristina Constantine the Great Airport LYPR/PRN

SLOVAKIA
Bratislava M R Stefanik Airport LZIB/BTS
Kosice Inernational Airport LZKZ/KSC

SLOVENIA
Ljubljana Joze Pucnik Airport LJLJ/LJU
Portorož Airport LJPZ/POW

SPAIN
A Coruña Airport LECO/LCG
Alicante Airport LEAL/ALC
Almeria Airport LEAM/LEI
Asturias Airport LEAS/OVD
Badajoz Airport LEBZ/BJZ
Barcelona El Prat Airport LEBL/BCN
Bilbao Airport LEBB/BIO
Ciudad Real Central Airport LERL/CQM
Fuertaventura El Matorral Airport GCFV/FUE
Girona-Costa Brava Airport LEGE/GRO
Granada/Jaen Federico Garcia Lorca Airport LEGR/GRX
Ibiza Airport LEIB/IBZ
Jerez Airport LEJR/XRY
La Palma Airport GCLA/SPC
Lanzarote Arrecife Airport GCRR/ACE
Las Palmas Gran Canaria GCLP/LPA
Leon Airport LELN/LEN
Lleida-Alguaire Airport LEDA/ILD
Madrid Barajas International Airport LEMD/MAD
Madrid Cuatros Vientos Airport LECU/MCV
Madrid Torrejon Airport LETO/TOJ
Malaga Airport LEMG/AGP

Melilla Airport GEML/MLN

Menorca Airport LEMH/MAH

Murcia-San Javier Airport LELC/MJV

Palma de Mallorca Airport LEPA/PMI

Pamplona-Noain Airport LEPP/PNA

Reus Airport LERS/REU

Salamanca Airport LESA/SLM

San Sebastian Airport LESO/EAS

Santander Airport LEXJ/SDR

Santiago de Compostela Airport LEST/SCQ

Seville Airport LEZL/SVQ

Tenerife North Los Rodeos Airport GCXO/TFN

Tenerife South Reina Sofia Airport GCTS/TFS

Valencia Airport LEVC/VLC

Valladolid Airport LEVD/VLL

Vigo-Peinador Airport LEVX/VGO

Vitoria Airport LEVT/VIT

Zaragoza Airport LEZG/ZAZ

SWEDEN

Ängelholm-Helsingborg Airport ESTA/AGH

Åre Östersund Airport ESNZ/OSD

Arvidsjaur Airport ESNX/AJR

Borlänge Airport ESSD/BLE

Gällivare Airport ESNG/GEV

Gothenburg City Airport EGSP/GSE

Gothenburg Landvetter Airport ESGG/GOT

Hagfors Airport ESOH/HFS

Halmstad Airport ESMT/HAD

Hemavan Airport ESUT/HMV

Jönköping Airport ESGJ/JKG

Kalmar Airport ESMQ/KLR

Karlstad Airport ESOK/KSD

Kiruna Airport ESNQ/KRN

Kramfors Airport ESNK/KRF

Kristianstad Airport ESMK/KID

Linköping Airport ESSL/LPI

Luleå Airport ESPA/LLA

Lycksele Airport ESNL/LYC

Malmö-Sturup Airport ESMS/MMX

Mora-Siljan Airport ESKM/MXX

Norrköping Airport ESSP/NRK

Örebro Airport ESOE/ORB

Örnsköldsvik Airport ESNO/OER

Oskarshamn Airport ESMO/OSK

Ronneby Airport ESDF/RNB

Skellefteå Airport ESNS/SFT

Stockholm-Arlanda Airport ESSA/ARN

Stockholm-Bromma Airport ESSB/BMA

Stockholm-Stavsta Airport ESKN/NYO

Stockholm-Västerås Airport ESOW/VST

Sundsvall-Härnösand Airport ESNN/SDL

Sveg Airport ESND/EVG

Torsby Airport ESST/TYF

Trollhättan-Vänersborg Airport ESGT/THN

Umeå Airport ESNU/UME

Växjö Airport ESMX/VXO

Vilhelmina Airport ESNV/VHM

Visby Airport ESSV/VBY

SWITZERLAND
Bern Airport LSZB/BRN

Geneva Cointrin International Airport LSGG/GVA

Lugano Airport LSZA/LUG

Sion Airport LSGS/SIR

St. Gallen-Altenrhein Airport LSZR/ACH

Zürich Kloten Airport LSZH/ZRH

TURKEY
Adana Şakirpaşa Airport LTAF/ADA

Ankara Esenboğa International Airport LTAC/ESB

Antakya Hatay Airport LTAK/HTY

Antalya Airport LTAI/AYT

Antalya Gazipaşa Airport LTGP/GZP

Balikesir Edremit Körfez Airport LTFD/EDO
Bodrum Milas Airport LTFE/BJV
Bursa Yenişehir Airport LTBR/YEI
Dalaman Airport LTBS/DLM
Erzurum Airport LTCE/ERZ
Eskişehir Anadolu Airport LTBY/AOE
Gaziantep Oğuzeli International Airport LTAJ/GZT
Istanbul Ataturk International Airport LTBA/IST
Istanbul Gökçen International Airport LTFJ/SAW
Izmir Menderes International Airport LTBJ/ADB
Kayseri Erkilet International Airport LTAU/ASR
Konya Airport LTAN/KYA
Malatya Erhac Airport LTAT/MLX
Nevşehir Kapadokya Airport LTAZ/NAV
Samsun-Çarşamba Airport LTFH/SZF
Trabzon Airport LTCG/TZX

UKRAINE
Chernivtsi International AirportUKKE/CKC
Dnipropetrovsk International Airport UKDD/DNK
Donetsk International Airport UKCC/DOK
Ivano-Frankivsk International Airport UKLI/IFO
Kharkiv International Airport UKHH/HRK
Kiev Boryspil International Airport UKBB/KBP
Kiev Zhuliany International Airport UKKK/IEV
Kryvyi Rih International Airport UKDR/KWG
Luhansk International Airport UKCW/VSG
Lviv International Airport UKLL/LWO
Mariupol International Airport UKCM/MPW
Odessa International Airport UKOO/ODS
Rivne International Airport UKLR/RWN
Sevastopol Belbek International Airport UKFB/UKS
Simferopol International Airport UKFF/SIP
Sumy Airport UKHS/UMY
Uzhhorod International Airport UKLU/UDJ
Zaporizhia International Airport UKDE/OZH

UNITED KINGDOM

Aberdeen Airport EGPD/ABZ

Alderney Airport EGJA/ACI

Belfast City "George Best" Airport EGAC/BHD

Belfast International Airport EGAA/BFS

Benbecula Airport EGPL/BEB

Biggin Hill Airport EGKB/BQH

Birmingham Airport EGBB/BHX

Blackpool International Airport EGNH/BLK

Bournemouth Airport EGHH/BOH

Bristol Airport EGGD/BRS

Cambridge Airport EGSC/CBG

Cardiff Airport EGFF/CWL

Chester Hawarden Airport EGNR/CEG

City of Derry Airport EGAE/LDY

Coventry Airport EGBE/CVT

Doncaster Sheffield "Robin Hood" Airport EGCN/DSA

Dundee Airport EGPN/DND

Durham Tees Valley Airport EGNV/MME

East Midlands Airport EGNX/EMA

Edinburgh Airport EGPH/EDI

Exeter International Airport EGTE/EXT

Farnborough Airport EGLF/FAB

Glasgow International Airport EGPF/GLA

Glasgow Prestwick International Airport EGPK/PIK

Gloucestershire Airport EGBJ/GLO

Guernsey Airport EGJB/GCI

Humberside Airport EGNJ/HUY

Inverness Airport EGPE/INV

Isle of Man Airport EGNS/IOM

Jersey Airport EGJJ/JER

Kirkwall Airport EGPA/KOI

Leeds Bradford International Airport EGNM/LBA

Liverpool John Lennon Airport EGGP/LPL

London City Airport EGLC/LCY

London Gatwick Airport EGKK/LGW

London Heathrow Airport EGLL/LHR
London Luton Airport EGGW/LTN
London Southend Airport EGMC/SEN
London Stansted Airport EGSS/STN
Lydd Airport EGMD/LYX
Manchester Airport EGCC/MAN
Manston Kent International Airport EGMH/MSE
Newcastle Airport EGNT/NCL
Newquay Cornwall Airport EGHQ/NQY
Norwich International Airport EGSH/NWI
Southampton Airport EGHI/SOU
Stornoway Airport EGPO/SYY
Sumburgh Airport EGPB/LSI
Tiree Airport EGPU/TRE
Wick Airport EGPC/WIC

VATICAN CITY
No Fixed Wing Airports

This page has been intentionally left blank.

Storage Airports by Country

Whilst Europe doesn't have the advantageous warm and dry climate of the western United States that suits the long-term storage of airliners, there are nevertheless a number of airports around Europe where aircraft storage and scrapping takes place. These include:

Chateauroux, France
Always a mixed bag of larger airliners in storage, although quieter in recent years. Aircraft are usually scrapped here.

Lourdes, France
A relatively new storage airport, housing widebody Airbus aircraft retired by the likes of Virgin Atlantic.

Perpignan, France
A small airport beside the main road which has some older types in storage, such as Boeing 727s and 737s.

Dresden, Germany
A number of retired aircraft pass through here for cargo conversions before moving on to new carriers.

Shannon, Ireland
Many aircraft come here for a change of identity, and often stay in storage for a while.

Woensdrecht, Netherlands
A storage and rework facility for Fokker aircraft.

Bucharest Baneasa, Romania
A small area of long-term storage of some older airliners can be found here.

Moscow Domodedovo, Russia
Many retired Russian types such as IL-62, IL-86, TU-134 and TU-154 are stored here following their retirement.

Madrid Barajas, Spain
Many aircraft formerly in use with Iberia sit outside their maintenance hangars awaiting scrapping.

Istanbul Sabiha Gökçen

There are usually plenty of stored cargo airliners at Istanbul's second airport.

Exeter, United Kingdom

Embraer aircraft are reworked and stored here, as well as the comings and goings of Flybe's fleet.

Kemble, United Kingdom

A busy scrapping airport in south-west England. Easy to view the lineup which also includes long-term storage and rework facilities.

Lasham, United Kingdom

A rework facility with some long-term residents, hidden in southern England near Farnborough.

London Southend, United Kingdom

Easily reached from London. A lot of airliners are stored, re-sprayed and tested here. Some are WFU in long-term storage.

Manston Kent, United Kingdom

An airport to the south of London which has some DC-8, Boeing 707 and 747 aircraft in long-term storage.

Norwich, United Kingdom

A mixture of rework, re-spray and storage of airlines, often those Fokker types, and aircraft from KLM.

European Airport Statistics

Europe is a continent of such diversity. It has been involved in flight since the earliest days, with many of the world's oldest airport still in operation here, and the Netherlands claiming the world's oldest airline (KLM) still in operation.

There are many thousands of airports in use in Europe. The tables below indicate the top ten airports in a variety of categories. Many of these are also amongst the top ten in the world for the same categories.

Busiest By Passengers

Airport		2010 Passengers
1.	London Heathrow, UK	65,881,660
2.	Paris Charles de Gaulle, France	58,164,612
3.	Frankfurt/Main, Germany	53,009,221
4.	Madrid Barajas, Spain	49,866,113
5.	Amsterdam Schiphol, Netherlands	45,211,749
6.	Rome Leonardo da Vinci Fiumicino, Italy	36,337,050
7.	Munich, Germany	34,721,605
8.	Istanbul Atatürk, Turkey	32,143,819
9.	London Gatwick, UK	31,375,290
10.	Barcelona El Prat, Spain	29,209,536

Busiest By Aircraft Movements

Airport		2010 Total Movements
1.	Paris Charles de Gaulle, France	499,997
2.	Frankfurt/Main, Germany	464,432
3.	London Heathrow, UK	454,883
4.	Madrid Barajas, Spain	433,683
5.	Amsterdam Schiphol, Netherlands	402,372

Busiest By Cargo

Airport
1. Paris Charles de Gaulle, France
2. Frankfurt/Main, Germany
3. London Heathrow, UK
4. Amsterdam Schiphol, Netherlands
5. Luxembourg-Findel

Airports in Austria

1. Salzburg
2. Vienna

This page has been intentionally left blank.

Salzburg W A Mozart Airport, Austria

SZG | LOWS

Tel: +43 662 85800
Web: www.salzburg-airport.com
Passengers: 1,552,154 (2009)

Overview

Salzburg is quite a small airport, situated amongst the hills next to the city, and quite close to the German border. For most of the year it is fairly quiet, but during the winter months it comes alive due to the skiing season.

Of particular interest is a period around December and January when Russians flock to the city in droves, using a variety of airlines rarely seen elsewhere in Europe. Whilst the number of older Soviet aircraft operating on these flights has now diminished, making way for less interesting Airbus and Boeing types, it is still nevertheless a good time to visit.

The airport has a single runway, and a number of spotting locations around the perimeter. You can take photographs with some stunning backgrounds if you are in the right position.

Spotting Locations

1. Terminal Terrace

Inside the terminal there is a staircase onto a viewing terrace next to the Panorama Market Place restaurant. This is ideal for seeing any aircraft parked at the terminal and using the runway. It's also perfectly acceptable for photographs at closer range.

2. Spotter Hill

Walk past Terminal 2 and the hangar next to it, and follow the footpath. It will lead to this spot which is next to the parking apron and taxiway. You can take good photographs and see all movements from here.

3. Runway 34

This spot is on the north side of the runway close to the taxiway and hold point. You can get good shots of aircraft on the ground and on final approach with a nice backdrop of castle and mountains. From the airport exit off the motorway, turn right after the lights on Loiger Strasse and turn right at the end. Turn left

MAP

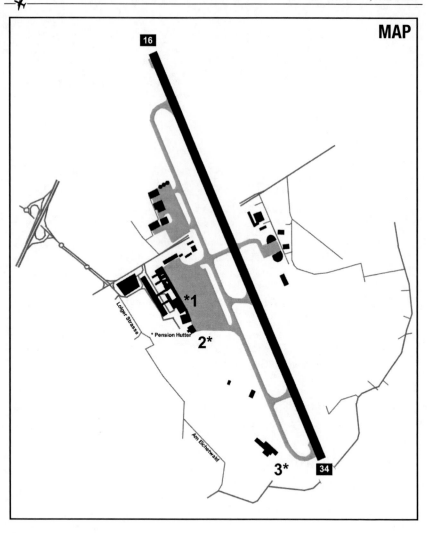

Frequencies

Tower	118.1
Ground	121.75
ATIS	125.725
Approach	123.725
Approach	134.975

Runways

16/34   9,022ft / 2,750m

onto Hermann Gmainer Strasse, then left onto Am Eichetwald. Turn left opposite the graveyard, and right at the junction. You will then come across the spot.

Airlines

Aer Lingus
Aeroflot
Air Berlin
Air VIA
Austrian Airlines (Lauda Air)
Austrian Arrows
British Airways
Cimber Sterling
Cirrus Airlines
easyJet
Estonian Air
Europe Airpost
Flybe
Germanwings
Jet2
Jettime
Kavminvodyavia
Malmo Aviation
Monarch
Niki
Norwegian Air Shuttle
Rossiya
Ryanair
Sky Airlines
Sky Express
SunExpress
TAROM
Thomas Cook Airlines
Thomson Airways
Transaero Airways
Transavia
Tunisair
Ukraine International Airlines
VIM Airlines
Vladivostok Air
Wind Rose Aviation
Yamal Airlines

Hotels

Pension Hutter

Dr.-Matthias-Laireiterstr.7, A-5020 Salzburg | +43 (0) 662 850 031 | www.pension-hutter.at

A small family-run pension close to Salzburg Airport's terminal. The owners are used to aviation enthusiasts and can usually provide a room facing the airport, from where movements can be seen.

Nearby Attractions

There are no aviation attractions in the immediate vicinity of Salzburg, however the airports at Linz and Innsbruck are around 65 and 90 miles away respectively. These can be reached easily by car or train.

Vienna International Airport, Austria

VIE | LOWW

Tel: +43 1 7007 0
Web: www.viennaairport.com
Passengers: 19,691,206 (2010)

Overview

Vienna's airport at Schwechat was constructed around a year before the start of World War 2 just as Germany took control of Austria and Lufthansa became the national carrier. During the war the Heinkel company took over the airport to conduct flight testing of its new aircraft. The first hard runway was laid for this purpose, and the Allied forces inflicted serious damage to it on numerous occasions.

Following the war the airport was rebuilt for civilian use by the Allied occupation force. However, it was not until 1953 that the airport saw any significant growth. Then, under the control of local authorities, the runway was extended and a new terminal built. In 1977 a second runway was opened to cope with increased traffic, and a new freight centre was opened in 1986 to cope with extra demand from cargo flights.

Today Vienna's airport handles primarily scheduled traffic to the main business and leisure destinations around Europe, North America, the Middle East and Asia. Austrian Airlines and its subsidiaries provide the majority of flights, with much of their fleet passing through the airport on any given day.

For spotters, a few locations exist and frustrating runway switches take place regularly, so be ready to move!

Spotting Locations

1. Terminal

The Balloon Café/Restaurant in the terminal's International Marketplace is the primary place to get views of movements. Most traffic will pass this spot either on the way in or out, however it is quite restrictive. Photographers will not like the tinted glass.

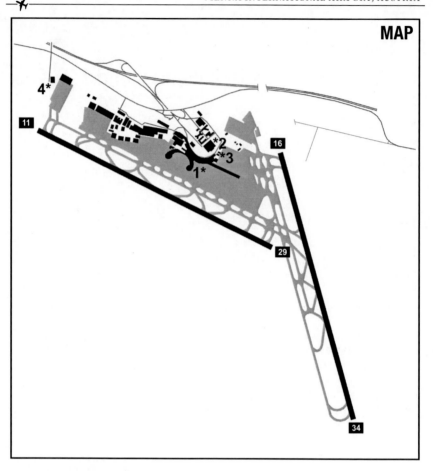

MAP

Frequencies

Tower	121.2
Tower	123.8
Info	118.525
Ground	121.6
Ground	121.77
Director	119.8
Director	126.55
Clearance Delivery	122.125
ATIS Departure	121.725
ATIS Arrival	122.95
Radar	124.55
Radar	128.2
Radar	129.05
Radar	132.475

Runways

11/29 11,483ft / 3,500m
16/34 11,811ft / 3,600m

2. Car Park P4

The top level of the multi-storey car park number 4 is situated alongside Runway 16/34. This is particularly good for logging and photographing aircraft using the 16 direction. You will also see a remote parking area alongside this car park which is hard to see from anywhere else. However, the new terminal extension partly obscures the view from this car park now. Car Park P3 also has views from the top floor.

3. Airport Tour

An airside tour is available from the VisitAir Centre adjacent to Car Park 4, which takes in the maintenance, general aviation, executive and passenger aprons. A security check is required. Tickets cost €8 for adults, less for children/concessions. The tour departs on the hour from 8.30am to 6pm, and lasts 50 minutes. Reservations required, on +43 17 00 72 21 50 or visitaircenter@viennaairport.com

4. Bizjet Ramp

Drive from the terminal towards Wien and then Schwechat, but don't use the motorway. Turn left at the airport exit, then turn left at the second set of lights. Park in the GA Terminal car park, and then walk towards the fence. You will see the parking ramp. A set of steps would be useful.

Airlines

Adria Airways	Austrian Airlines	EgyptAir
Aegean Airlines	(Lauda Air)	El Al
Aer Lingus	Austrian Arrows	EVA Air
Aeroflot	bmi British Midland	Farnair Hungary
Air Berlin	British Airways	FedEx Express
Air China Cargo	Brussels Airlines	Finnair
Air Dolomiti	Bulgaria Air	Freebird Airlines
Air France	Bulgarian Air Charter	Georgian Airways
Air Malta	Central Connect Airlines	Germanwings
Air Moldova	China Airlines	Hamburg Airways
Air Transat	China Southern	Iberia
Air VIA	Airlines Cargo	InterSky
airBaltic	Cirrus Airlines	Iran Air
Alitalia	Condor	Jat Airways
Alitalia (Air One)	Croatia Airlines	KLM
Arkia Israel Airlines	DHL Aviation	KLM CityHopper
Asiana Cargo	easyJet	Korean Air
Austrian Airlines	Emirates	Korean Air Cargo

LOT Polish Airlines
LOT (EuroLOT)
Lufthansa
Lufthansa Regional
Lufthansa Regional
(Eurowings)
Luxair
Montenegro Airlines
Niki
Norwegian Air Shuttle
Pegasus Airlines
Pegasus Airlines (IZair)

People's Viennaline
Qatar Airways
Rossiya
Royal Jordanian
Sky Airlines
Sky Work Airlines
SunExpress
Syrian Air
Swiss International
Air Lines
TAP Portugal
TAROM

TNT Airways
Transaero Airlines
Transavia
Tunisair
Turkish Airlines
Turkish Airlines
(Anadolujet)
Ukraine International
UPS Airlines
Ural Airlines
Vueling

Hotels

NH Vienna Airport Hotel

Einfahrtsstrasse 1-3, Wien Flughafen 1300 | +43 1 70 15 10 | www.nh-hotels.com

The best hotel at Vienna Airport for views of movements. Odd-numbered rooms on the third floor will give views over the apron. Some other higher rooms have views over the 11/29 runway. The hotel is one of the more affordable at the airport, and it is a short walk from the terminal.

Nearby Attractions

Bratislava Airport

Despite being in another country's capital, Bratislava is only around 30 miles from Vienna. As such, it's easy to make a side trip to the airport. It is much quieter these days, handling a few low-cost and holiday airlines, and cargo flights from DHL. A path runs alongside the perimeter fence, giving good views of aircraft on the 31/13 runway.

Airports in Belgium

1. Brussels
2. Liege

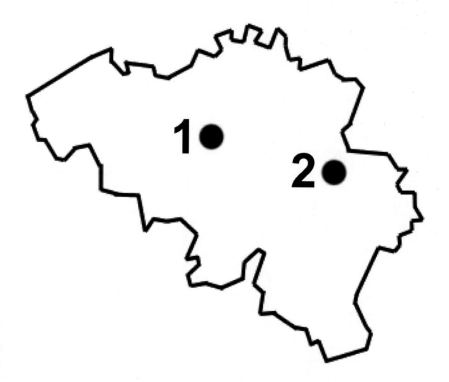

This page has been intentionally left blank.

Brussels National Airport, Belgium

BRU | EBBR

Tel: +32 2 753 77 53
Web: www.brusselsairport.be
Passengers: 17,180,606 (2010)

Overview

Brussels is the largest and busiest airport in Belgium, serving the capital and headquarters of the European Union. It continues to fare well in terms of passenger throughput with many airlines and cargo carriers, especially since Brussels Airlines has grown into a good replacement for SABENA, and also since Jet Airways set up a long-haul hub at the airport.

The reorganisation of the national carrier has seen a number of changes at the airport, and interesting airlines to see operating the principal routes throughout Europe, and to North America and Africa. Most of the important carriers, both local and long-haul, serve Brussels. Low-cost carriers are not as prevalent.

Cargo was always important to Brussels, with FedEx and DHL traditionally having bases here. This has changed somewhat since the early 1990s, and there are now fewer cargo operations here. You may still catch unusual freighters from far-off parts, however.

The airport doesn't provide any official spotting locations, however there are a number of locations where movements can be logged – especially for those with a car. Airside, the airport is very good for spotting.

Spotting Locations

1. Car Park

Walk outside the terminal and head to the left, where the multi-storey car park can be found. The top level gives views over the southern apron and hangar areas. Photography is possible from here.

2. Water Tower

The road running around the perimeter has a spot close to the end of Runway 25L which offers good shots of landings and aircraft on the runway. It is so named because of the nearby water tower. To reach the location, take the A201 motorway away from the terminal, and the R0 motorway south. Leave this after a few miles

MAP

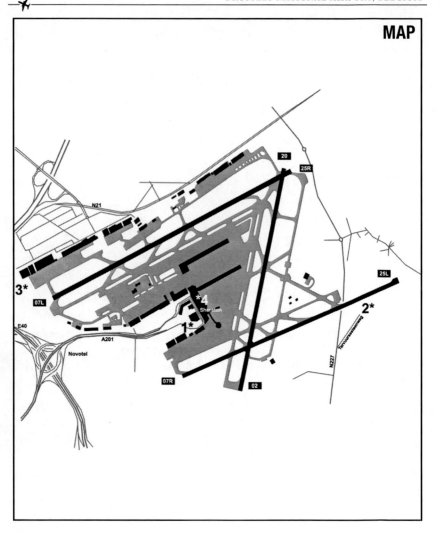

Frequencies

Tower	120.775
Ground	118.05
Ground	121.7
Ground	121.875
Departures	126.625
Clearance Delivery	121.95
ATIS Arrival	132.475
Approach	118.25
Approach	120.1
Approach	122.5

Runways

02/20	9,800ft / 2,987m
07L/25R	11,936ft / 3,638m
07R/25L	10,535ft / 3,211m

for the E20 East. Take the first exit left on to Mechelsesteenweg (N227). Before the tunnel under the runway, turn right on to Tervuursesteenweg. You will see parked cars and spotters at the end of the runway.

3. Cargo Area

Following directions for the General Aviation Area, taking another left and following the road. Turn right in the direction of Haacht on the N21. Turn right at the second traffic lights, following Cargo signs. Go right at the roundabout and left at the Post building. Turn right after 100m and park next to the security gate. A short walk reveals the parked cargo aircraft at close quarters. Some pictures of aircraft taxiing are possible.

4. Wingtips Restaurant

The spotting location recommended by the airport itself is the Wingtips Restaurant, located on the fourth floor of the terminal, which is not airside. There are fairly panoramic views over the central apron area here, and many aircraft will taxi past. Photography is possible. Some aircraft will not be seen from here, particularly on the cargo ramps.

Airlines

Adria Airways	Blue Air	Estonian Air
Aegean Airlines	Blue1	Ethiopian Airlines
Aer Lingus	bmi Regional	Etihad Airways
Aeroflot	British Airways	EVA Air Cargo
Aerologic	British Airways (Sun Air)	FedEx Feeder (Air
Air Algerie	Brussels Airlines	Contractors)
Air Arabia Maroc	Brussels Airlines	Finnair
Air Canada	(bmi Regional)	Flybe
Air France (Regional)	Bulgaria Air	Freebird Airlines
Air Lipsia (Central	Bulgarian Air Charter	Gestair
Connect Airlines)	Cathay Pacific Cargo	Global Aviation &
Air Malta	Corendon Airlines	Services Group
Air Transat	Croatia Airlines	Hainan Airlines
airBaltic	Czech Airlines	Iberia
Alitalia	Delta Air Lines	Iberia (Air Nostrum)
American Airlines	Demavia Airlines	Icelandair
Aryan Cargo Express	DHL Airways	Jat Airways
Asiana Cargo	easyJet	Jet Airways
Atlas Air	easyJet Switzerland	Jetairfly
Austrian Airlines	EgyptAir	Kalitta Air
Austrian Arrows	EgyptAir Cargo	KLM Cityhopper
Belle Air	El Al	Korean Air Cargo

LOT Polish Airlines	Saudi Arabian	Thomas Cook
Lufthansa	Airlines Cargo	Airlines Belgium
Lufthansa Regional	Scandinavian Airlines	TNT Airways
Lydd Air	Singapore Airlines Cargo	Tunisair
Malev	Sky Airlines	Turkish Airlines
Middle East Airlines	Swiss European Air Lines	Turkish Airlines
Nouvelair	Swiss International	(Anadolujet)
OLT	Air Lines	Ukraine International
Onur Air	Syrian Air	Airlines
Pegasus Airlines	Tailwind Airlines	United Airlines
Qatar Airways	TAP Portugal	US Airways
Royal Air Maroc	TAP Portugal (Portugalia)	Vueling
Royal Jordanian	TAROM	
Royal Joranian Cargo	Thai Airways International	

Hotels

Sheraton Brussels Airport
Brussels National Airport, Brussels 1930 | +32 27 10 80 00 | www.sheraton.com

This is the best hotel option for spotting aircraft at Brussels Airport. Although expensive, rooms have views over the aprons. It is a short walk from the terminal and multi-storey car park location. Photography is not possible from the rooms, however.

Novotel Brussels Airport
Da Vinci Laan 25, Bedrijvenzone Diegem-Vuurberg, Diegem 1831 | +32 27 25 30 50 | www.novotel.com

Affordable hotel, located less than 2km from the terminals, with free shuttles. Rooms on higher floors have good views, and it is also located a short distance from the Runway 18 spot.

Nearby Attractions

Musée Royal de l'Armée
Jubelpark 3, Brussels 1000 | +32 (0) 27 37 78 33 | www.klm-mra.be

A museum in the Parc de Cinquantenaire in downtown Brussels which has a number of aircraft on display. These include a Boeing 707 (nose section) and Sud Aviacion Caravelle formerly of SABENA, plus a DC-3 and a Junkers Ju-52. Open Tuesday to Sunday 9am to 12pm and 1pm to 4.45pm. Admission free.

Brussels-Charleroi Airport
The local low-cost airport, and a base for Ryanair. Charleroi is 28 miles from Brussels. Buses run regularly from the city centre. There are some spotting locations around the airport and terminal.

Liege Airport
See separate entry.

Liege Airport, Belgium

LGG | EBLG

Tel: +32 4 234 84 11
Web: www.liegeairport.com
Passengers: 299,043 (2010)

Overview

Despite being only a modest sized regional airport, Liege has positioned itself as one of Europe's leading cargo airports. It is often a compulsory stop off for spotters driving into Europe from the UK due to its convenient location.

The airport is a hub for TNT Airways, and is also served by a number of other cargo airlines. Passenger airlines mostly focus on summer charters to the sun.

To make the most of seeing cargo aircraft, be here late at night. Most movements are during the early hours, with departures starting at 4am. If you visit during the day you may still see a number of aircraft parked on the ramp, and some others operating in or out.

Spotting Locations

1. TNT Parking Lot

Alongside the TNT building is a parking lot from which you can get views and photographs of aircraft landing in both directions, as well as aircraft on the taxiway. You will need a step ladder for the best shots. Beware that you will likely be moved on if you get too close to the fence.

2. Runway 23

Construction work on the roads around the runway 23 extension means you can park at the closed exit from the roundabout here, but beware of security cameras. Walk from the car to the small hill which gives great views of aircraft landing and on the runway/taxiway. You'll need a stepladder to get shots over the fence.

A further hill is located on the northern side, which can be used when the sun has moved round later in the day.

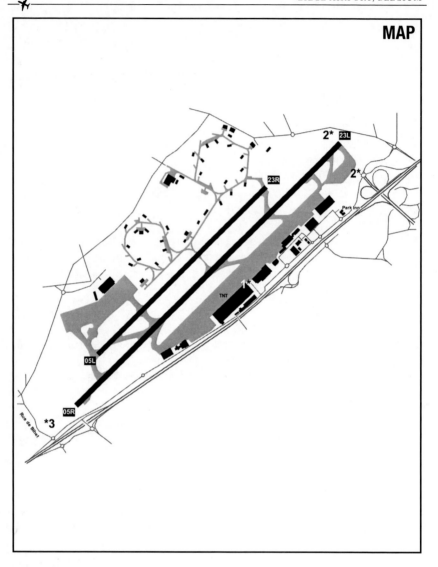

Frequencies

Tower	122.1
Tower	130.625
Ground	121.925
Clearance Delivery	121.8
ATIS	115.45
ATIS	126.25
Approach	119.275
Approach	122.5

Runways
05L/23R 7,677ft / 2,340m
05R/23L 12,139ft / 3700m

3. Runway 05

There's a small car park alongside the road (Rue de Bihet) here which allows you to park up and get shots of aircraft landing on runway 05. You can also see through the fence to aircraft on the ground, but can not photograph them.

Airlines

Africa West Airlines
Avient Aviation
Belle Air
CAL Cargo Airlines
El Al Cargo
Ethiopian Airlines Cargo
FedEx Feeder (Air Contractors)
Freebird Airlines
Icelandair Cargo
Kalitta Air
Jetairfly
Nightexpress
Nouvelair
Southern Air
Thomas Cook Airlines Belgium
TNT Airways
TNT Airways (ABX Air)
TNT Airways (Ukraine International)
Tunisair

Hotels

Park Inn Liege Airport

14 Rue de l'Aéroport, Bâtiment 14 - 4460 Liège | +32 (0) 4 241 00 00 | www.parkinn.nl/arporthotel-liege

This hotel is very close to the airport terminal and has rooms overlooking the freight ramp from the third floor upwards. It's an ideal base to watch night time cargo movements, and not too expensive.

Nearby Attractions

Maastricht/Aachen Airport

A regional airport (located in the Netherlands) 25 miles from Liege which handles a few low cost and holiday airlines. Like Liege, it is also fairly busy with cargo flights by a number of interesting airlines. There are a variety of places to spot around the perimeter of the airport.

This page has been intentionally left blank.

Airports in Czech Republic

1. Prague

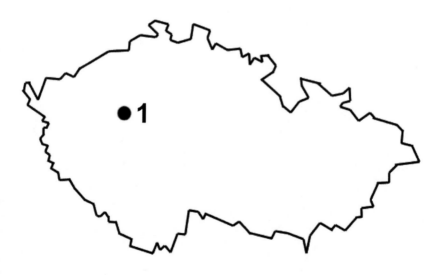

This page has been intentionally left blank.

Prague Airport, Czech Republic

PRG | LKPR

Tel: +420 220 111 888
Web: www.prg.aero
Passengers: 11,643,366 (2009)

Overview

Prague is one of the busier airports in Eastern Europe. It experienced a boom in the early 2000s as low-cost carriers flocked in to provide cheap city break and stag/bachelor party trips from the UK in particular. Today things have settled down more, but it's still a good place to visit for the spotter, even if the days of Russian aircraft flying in are long gone.

The airport has two active runways and three terminals. Terminals 1 and 2 are the main passenger ones, whilst Terminal 3 is for VIPs and executive flights, and located a little further away.

Spotting opportunities are quite good, and there's a strong local community who keep the hobby alive. As with many airports, there is an extended police presence when the El Al flight arrives. Otherwise, you will rarely be bothered if you stay within the law.

Spotting Locations

1. Terminal Viewing Area

Between Terminals 1 and 2 is a small viewing area on the roof. It looks out over piers B and C, and the main runway 06/24 ahead. You will see most movements from here, but will miss anything parked out of sight.

2. Car Parks

The various car parks outside the terminal offer good views from the top levels. It is usually no problem to be there, and by moving around you will see aircraft parked away from the terminal gates. There is also a preserved DC-3 nearby. It's not perfect for photography, but some shots are possible.

MAP

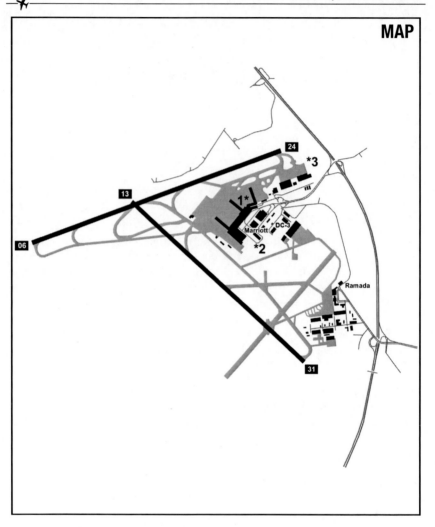

Frequencies

Tower	119.7
Radar	119.0
Ground	118.1
Ground	121.9
Info	118.3
Clearance Delivery	120.05
ATIS	122.15
Approach	120.525
Approach	127.575
Approach	136.075

Runways

06/24	12,191ft / 3,715m
13/31	10,665ft / 3,250m

3. Runway 24

You can walk or drive from the terminal area to a couple of good spots for aircraft using runway 24. Head towards the Menzies Aviation area (where you might see some aircraft on the ground), and walk towards the fence. Different spots are good for aircraft on approach, and aircraft lining up on the runway.

Airlines

Aer Lingus
Aeroflot
Aerosvit Airlines
Air Arabia Egypt
Air Cairo
Air Contractors
Air France
Air France (Brit Air)
Air Malta
Alitalia (Air One)
Austrian Arrows
Azerbaijan Airlines
Belavia
bmibaby
British Airways
Brussels Airlines
Bulgaria Air
Central Connect Airlines
China Airlines Cargo
Cimber Sterling
City Airline
Cyprus Airways
Czech Airlines
Delta Air Lines
Donavia
easyJet
El Al
Emirates
Finnair
Freebird Airlines
Genex
Germanwings
Hi Fly

Holidays Czech Airlines
Iberia
Jet2
KLM Cityhopper
Korean Air
LOT Polish Airlines
Lufthansa
Lufthansa Regional
Lufthansa Regional (Augsburg Airlines)
Luxair
Malev
Norwegian Air Shuttle
Nouvelair
OLT Jetair
Onur Air
Rossiya
S7 Airlines
Scandinavian Airlines
Smart Wings
Swiss European Air Lines
Swiss (Contact Air)
Tailwind Airlines
TAP Portugal
Tatarstan Airlines
TNT Airways
Transavia
Travel Service
Tunis Air
Turkish Airlines
UPS Airlines (Farnair Switzerland)
Ural Airlines
Vueling
Wind Jet

Wizz Air

Yakutia Airlines

Yamal Airlines

Yangtze River Express

Hotels

Ramada Prague Airport

K Letisti 25a 1067 Prague, 16000 | +420 220 111 250 | www.ramada.com

Located near Terminal 3 at the airport. This is not a tall hotel, but some rooms face towards the airport and you will see movements. A request to the staff when checking in should help you get the best options.

Courtyard by Marriott

Aviatická 1092/8, 161 00 Prague 6 | +420 236 077 077 | www.marriott.com

Situated close to terminals 1 and 2. This is a smart hotel, but not very large. As such, the view is somewhat blocked by the surrounding buildings. Some rooms may offer views of aircraft on approach or departure, so a SBS unit or web flight tracker would be useful.

Nearby Attractions

National Technical Museum

Kostelní 42, 170 78 Praha 7 | +420 220 399 111 | www.ntm.cz

A museum covering various technical aspects in central Prague. Its Transport collection covers aviation, cars, boats and trains from a Czech Republic perspective. There are around 20 aircraft on display, including a Supermarine Spitfire. Open Tuesday-Sunday and public holidays from 10am-6pm. Tickets cost CZK360 (Adult), CZK230 (Concessions) and CZK850 (Family).

Kbely Aviation Museum

www.vhu.cz/en/stranka/letecke-muzeum/

Situated at the Prague-Kbely airfield, this museum has a large collection of aircraft preserved and on display over four halls and the outdoor area. It is particularly focussed on Czech aviation and military history. Museum is open Tuesday-Sunday from 10am-6pm (May-October and special days only). Admission is free. To get to the museum take bus No. 185, 259, 280, 302, 375, 376 - 10 minutes from Letnany underground station (stop Letecké museum).

1. Copenhagen

This page has been intentionally left blank.

Copenhagen Airport, Denmark

CPH I EKCH

Tel: +32 31 32 31
Web: www.cph.dk
Passengers: 21,501,750 (2010)

Overview

Copenhagen is one of Europe's oldest airports. It became popular as a hub early in its career with the formation of Scandinavian Airline System (SAS), and the introduction of trans-polar flights from America. Today it is one of the busiest airports in Scandinavia.

Perched at the southern end of the city on a peninsula, Copenhagen Airport has three runways but is surrounded by residential areas and the coast.

The airport has three terminals. Terminal 1 handles all domestic flights; Terminal 2 handles most of the general traffic at the airport, and most international airlines; Terminal 3 is used by SAS and its Star Alliance partners for international flights – by far the busiest users of the airport. A number of cargo airlines use the airport's facilities also.

Copenhagen has a few locations for watching aircraft, however it is regarded as a fairly frustrating airport for those without a boarding pass.

Spotting Locations

1. Flyvergrillen

By far the most popular spotting location at Copenhagen is located alongside Runway 22R/04L. The Flyvergrillen is a café and burger bar, and has a dirt mound alongside which offers views over the movements on the runways and taxiways. It is acceptable for photography on afternoons. To reach the spot, walk out of Terminal 1 and turn left at the catering buildings. You can also drive this route. It takes 30 minutes to walk.

2. Runway 22L

From Terminal 3, walk to the right. At the roundabout with McDonalds and the filling station, turn right and walk past the DHL buildings. Follow the path round past the end of the runway until you reach a suitable spot. This location is good

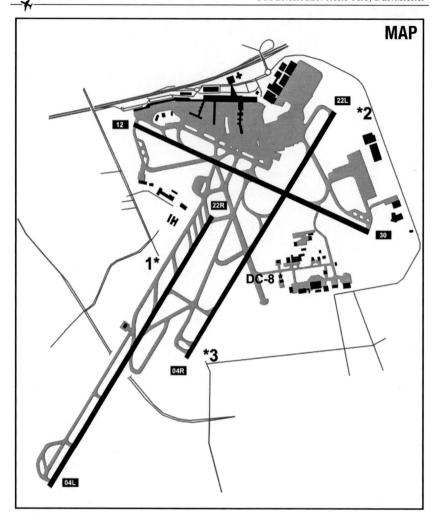

Frequencies

Tower	118.7
Tower	119.35
Taxi	118.575
Taxi	121.825
Ground Arrivals	121.65
Ground	121.725
Ground	121.9
Clearance Delivery	119.9
ATIS Arrival	122.75
ATIS Departure	122.85
Approach	119.8

Runways

04L/22R 11,811ft / 3,600m
04R/22L 10,827ft / 3,300m
12/30 9,186ft / 2,800m

for photographs of aircraft on short finals on mornings and early afternoons. You will also be able to log aircraft at all terminals and the cargo area.

3. Runway 04R

A good spot can be reached by car when aircraft are using Runway 04R. Follow the road away from the terminals and past the Flyvergrillen spot. Eventually, join Englandsvej southbound and go through the tunnel under the airport. After emerging at the other side, take the first left on to Nordre Kinkelgade. Follow this to the left through the small village, and eventually you will come to the spot alongside the fence. A stepladder is required for good shots. Aircraft at the terminals are too far away to accurately read off.

Airlines

Adria Airways
Aeroflot
Aerosvit Airlines
airBaltic
Air Berlin
Air Canada
Air China Cargo
Air France
Air France (Brit Air)
Air Greenland
Air Greenland (Jettime)
Alitalia
Arkia Israel Airlines
Atlantic Airways
Austrian Airlines
Austrian Arrows
B&H Airlines
Blue1
Blue1 (Golden Air)
bmi Regional
British Airways
British Airways
(BA Cityflyer)
Brussels Airlines
China Cargo Airlines
Cimber Sterling
Croatia Airlnes
Czech Airlines
Delta Air Lines

DHL Aviation
DHL Aviation (Exin)
easyJet
easyJet Switzerland
EgyptAir
Emirates
Estonian Air
FedEx Express
Finnair
Germanwings
Gulf Air
Iberia
Iceland Express
Icelandair
Iran Air
Jat Airways
Karthago Airlines
KLM
Korean Air Cargo
LOT Polish Airlines
Lufthansa
Malev
Malmo Aviation
Middle East Airlines
Montenegro Airlines
NextJet
Niki
Norwegian Air Shuttle
Novair

Pakistan International
Airlines
Pegasus Airlines
Primera Air
Qatar Airways
Rossiya
SATA International
Scandinavian Airlines
Singapore Airlines
Singapore Airlines Cargo
Sky Airlines
Skyways Express
Spanair
Swiss European Air Lines
Swiss International
Air Lines
Syrian Air
TAP Portugal
Thai Airways International
Thomas Cook Airlines
Scandinavia
TUIfly Nordic
Turkish Airlines
Turkish Airlines
(Anadolujet)
United Airlines
Wideroe
Wind Jet

Hotels

Hilton Airport Hotel
Ellehammersvej 20, Copenhagen 2770 | +45 32 50 15 01 | www.hilton.com

The Hilton is linked to the terminal via a covered walkway. Most even-numbered rooms from the 10th floor up offer views of the aprons, with photography possible. Can be expensive.

Zleep Airport Hotel
Englandsvej 333, Copenhagen 2770 | www.zleephotels.com

Although it offers no views of aircraft from its rooms, this hotel is very affordable and only a short walk from both the terminal and the café viewing area.

Nearby Attractions

Malmö Sturup Airport

Despite being over the border in Sweden, Malmö is very close to Copenhagen and just a short drive across the impressive Oresund Bridge. The airport is used extensively by low-cost carriers such as Cimber Sterling and Wizz Air. It is also served by Malmö Aviation and SAS. There are limited views from the terminal and car parks of aircraft on the ground. A Caravelle can be found on the fire dump.

Airports in Finland

1. Helsinki

This page has been intentionally left blank.

Helsinki Vantaa Airport, Finland

HEL | EFHK

Tel: +358 200 14636
Web: www.helsinki-vantaa.fi
Passengers: 12,884,500 (2010)

Overview

Finland has always had a strong association with aviation. The capital, Helsinki, is today a fairly busy hub for the national carrier and handles a number of flights from across Europe, North America, the Middle and Far East. In addition to this, a healthy cargo operation takes place at the airport.

The airport at Vantaa was opened in 1952 for the Helsinki Olympics. It replaced the older facility at Malmi, which today is used as the city's general aviation airport. A number of expansion projects are underway at Vantaa to help the airport cope with future growth.

The weather can often put a dampener on spending time at Helsinki, but long hours of sunlight in the summer months also prove advantageous. When the weather is against you, the café in the International Terminal provides a warm location with excellent views.

Whilst most of Europe's airlines visit Helsinki, its proximity to former Soviet and Baltic states means there's always something of interest passing through. Runway 22L is the most commonly used for movements due to the prevalent winds and noise abatement procedures, however runways can regularly be switched or used in parallel.

Spotting Locations

1. International Terminal Café

Located between halls 2 and 3 on the 3rd floor of the International Terminal (another café on the 2nd floor also has some views). The café has large windows fronting the aprons and the taxiways and runways. Most of the traffic will pass here at some point. Photography is possible, however the glass is usually dirty.

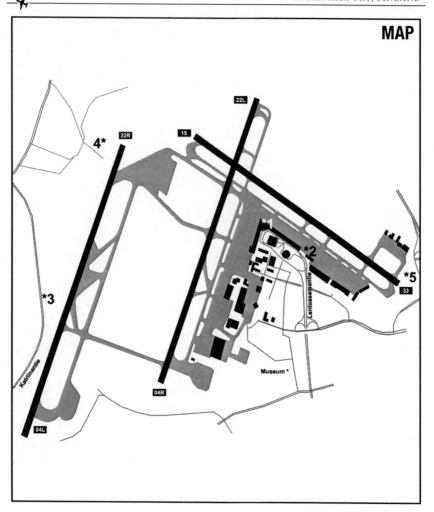

MAP

Frequencies

Tower	118.85
Tower	119.7
Ramp	121.65
Ground	121.8
Clearance Delivery	118.125
ATIS Departure	114.2
ATIS Arrival	135.075
Approach	119.1
Approach	119.9
Approach	124.325
Approach	129.85

Runways

04L/22R	10,039ft / 3,060m
04R/22L	11,286ft / 3,440m
15/33	9,518ft / 2,901m

2. Domestic Terminal

Outside the Domestic Terminal, walk to the right for 100m until you reach the ramp which allows you views over the movements. This is the best spot when runways 15 or 33 are in use, as traffic will taxi past you on the way in and out. Be warned that aircraft can park in front of you, rendering the spot of little use. Some views of the cargo apron and passenger gates are possible from here.

3. Runway 04L/22R

Exit the terminal area along Lentoasemantie and turn right at the traffic lights. Around 3km later, turn right at a T-junction and drive along Katriinantie until the runway comes into view. Try any of the gravel roads on the right. There are various spots along here which can lead to fantastic photographs when the runway is in use. Some sand hills give you an elevated view, but bring a ladder if you have one.

4. Runway 15

Exit the terminal area along Lentoasemantie and turn right at the traffic lights. Around 3km later, turn right at a T-junction and drive along Katriinantie, then follow sign Myllykylä/Kvarnbacken. Drive for 500m and turn right next to a billboard. Drive for 800m and turn right. Leave your car near the junction and walk to the left past a hill. This elevated spot gives great photos of aircraft on short finals to Runway 15.

5. Runway 33

Exit the terminal towards Kehä/Ring III, then take the first exit and turn left at the lights towards RAHTI. Then turn left towards RAHTI II. Turn left after 900m, passing the TNT building. Turn left at the T-junction and then park. The sand hills here have an elevated position with views over Runway 15/33 and the cargo ramps. Photography is possible of aircraft parked here, as well as those on the runway and taxiway. The sun can be a problem from late morning.

Airlines

Aer Lingus	Belavia	DHL Aviation (Exin)
Aeroflot	Blue1	FedEx Express
Air Aland (NextJet)	Blue1 (Golden Air)	Finnair
airBaltic	British Airways	Finnair (Finncomm
Air Berlin	British Airways (Sun Air)	Airlines)
Air Finland	Bulgaria Air	Finnair (Flybe Nordic)
American Airlines	City Airline	Finnair Cargo (Nordic
Austrian Arrows	Czech Airlines	Global Airlines)
Avies	DHL Aviation	Finnair Cargo

(World Airways)	Malev Hungarian Airlines	TAP Portugal
Finncomm Airlines	Nordavia	Thomas Cook Airlines
Flybe Nordic	Norwegian Air Shuttle	Scandinavia
Freebird Airlines	Nouvelair	TNT Airways
Gotlandsflyg	Primera Air	TUIfly Nordic
Icelandair	Qatar Airways	Turkish Airlines
KLM	Rossiya	Ukraine International
KLM CityHopper	Scandinavian Airlines	Airlines
LOT Polish Airlines	Spanair	UPS Airlines
Lufthansa	Sun Express	West Air Sweden

Hotels

Hilton Helsinki-Vantaa Airport

Lentajankuja 1, Vantaa 01530 | +358 97 32 22 211 | www.hilton.com

Situated at the terminal complex. Expensive hotel, but some higher rooms have views of aircraft movements.

Cumulus Airport Hotel

Robert Huberin Tie 4, Vantaa 01510 | +358 94 15 77 100

No reports of any rooms with views of movements, however the hotel has a number of floors and is only a short distance from the terminal area and the threshold of Runway 04R, so there is a possibility. The benefit of this hotel is that it's one of the more affordable at Vantaa.

Nearby Attractions

Finnish Aviation Museum

Helsinki-Vantaa Airport, Tietotie 3, 01539 VANTAA | +358 98 70 08 70 | www.suomenilumuseo.fi

This popular museum houses over 70 historic aircraft linked in some way to Finnish aviation history. Included are a Convair 440, DC-2 and a DC-3. It is open daily from 11am to 6pm. Adults E6, Children/Concessions E3

Helsinki Malmi Airport

Malmi Airport is the original Helsinki Airport. It has a well-preserved pre-war terminal building. Malmi is the city's general aviation airport. Ramp access can occasionally be granted, otherwise views are possible from the terminal area.

Airports in France

1. Paris Charles de Gaulle
2. Paris Orly
3. Toulouse

This page has been intentionally left blank.

Paris Charles de Gaulle Airport, France

CDG | LFPG

Tel: +33 1 70 36 39 50
Web: www.aeroportsdeparis.fr
Passengers: 58,164,612 (2010)

Overview

Charles de Gaulle, also known as Roissy, is the busiest airport in France and one of the busiest in Europe in terms of passenger numbers. In terms of movements and cargo it was Europe's busiest in 2006.

Charles de Gaulle is the main operating base for Air France, and a number of other French airlines. It handles flights from every corner of the globe, and across Europe. Surprisingly for such a busy airport, it also handles a number of low-cost airlines.

The original Terminal 1 is now fairly old and has a curious design. Nevertheless, it still handles most of the non-Air France traffic at the airport. Air France and its partners use Terminal 2, and the basic Terminal 3 is used by the low-cost and charter airlines. Large cargo facilities can be found to the west of both terminal areas, with the airport handling FedEx's main European distribution, and also Air France Cargo's operations. A number of other cargo airlines pass through.

France has made a name for itself in recent years for proving difficult with aviation enthusiasts. Despite a number of good locations, authorities have placed a ban on photography, and can be less than welcoming to spotters. It always helps to have a letter written in French explaining your plans.

To apply for a permit to photography at Paris, e-mail xavier.huby@seine-saint-denis.pref.gouv.fr

Spotting Locations

1. Mound

The classic spot at Charles de Gaulle where most spotters congregate to watch the action. Its raised position makes it fine for photography, and its location means most aircraft movements will at least be visible if not in close range for photographs. The spot is located alongside the Hilton hotel and train station between all three terminals, and easily reached by foot.

MAP

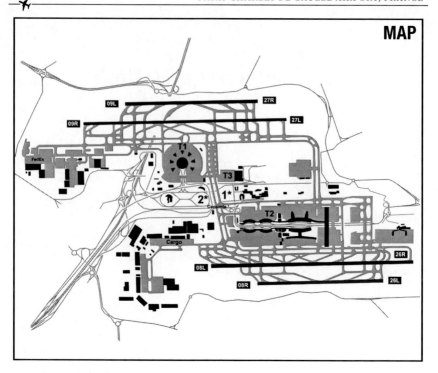

Frequencies

Tower	09/27	123.6
Tower	08/26	118.65
Tower	08/26	120.9
Tower	08/26	125.325
Pre Flight		121.725
Pre Flight		126.65
Ground North		121.6
Ground North		121.775
Ground South		121.8
Ground South		121.975
Departure		124.35
Departure		126.575
Departure		131.2
Departure		133.375
ATIS		127.125
Approach		118.15
Approach		119.85
Approach		121.5
Approach		125.825
Approach		126.425

Runways

08L/26R	13,829ft / 4,215m
08R/26L	8,858ft / 2,700m
09L/27R	8,858ft / 2,700m
09R/27L	13,780ft / 4,200m

2. Motorway Bridge

A little to the west of the first spot, and closer to Terminal 1 is the motorway bridge. From here aircraft can be seen taxiing. It is fine for photography. There are no views of Terminal 2, however.

Airlines

Adria Airways
Aegean Airlines
Aer Lingus
Aeroflot
Aeromexico
Afriqiyah Airways
Aigle Azur
Air Algerie
Air Arabia Maroc
Air Austral
Air Canada
Air China
Air China Cargo
Air Europa
Air France
Air France (Airlinair)
Air France (Brit Air)
Air France (CityJet)
Air France (Regional)
Air France Cargo
Air France Cargo (MNG Airlines)
Air India
Air Madagascar
Air Malta
Air Mauritius
Air Mediterranee
Air Moldova
Air Seychelles
Air Tahiti Nui
Air Transat
airBaltic
Alitalia
All Nippon Airways
American Airlines

Arkia Israel Airlines
Armavia
Asiana Airlines
Austrian Airlines
Azerbaijan Airlines
Belavia
Blue1
bmibaby
British Airways
Brussels Airlines
Bulgaria Air
Cargo Garuda Indonesia
Cathay Pacific
Cathay Pacific Cargo
Camairco
China Airlines Cargo
China Eastern Airlines
China Southern Airlines
Croatia Airlines
Cyprus Airways
Czech Airlines
Delta Air Lines
DHL
easyJet
easyJet Switzerland
EgyptAir
El Al
Emirates
Estonian Air
Ethiopian Airlines
Etihad Airways
Europe Airpost
EVA Air
FedEx Express

FedEx Feeder (Air Contractors)
Finnair
Flybe
Gabon Airlines
Georgian Airways
Gulf Air
Iceland Express
Icelandair
Itali Airlines
Japan Airlines
Jat Airways
Jet2
Kenya Airways
KLM
KLM CityHopper
Korean Air
Korean Air Cargo
Kuwait Airways
LOT Polish Airlines
Lufthansa
Lufthansa Regional
Lufthansa Regional (Eurowings)
Luxair
Malaysia Airlines
Malev
Mauritania Airlines International
Meridiana Fly
Middle East Airlines
Montenegro Airlines
MNG Airlines
Niki
Oman Air
Onur Air

Pakistan International Airlines
Qatar Airways
Rossiya
Royal Air Maroc
Royal Jordanian
Saudi Arabian Airlines
Scandinavian Airlines
Singapore Airlines
Smart Wings
SriLankan Airlines
Sunwing Airlines
Swiss International Air Lines
TACV
TAM Airlines
TAROM
Thai Airways International
TNT Airways
Trawel Fly
Tunisair
Turkish Airlines
Turkish Airlines Cargo
Ukraine International Airlines
United Airlines
UPS Airlines
UPS Airlines (Star Air)
US Airways
Uzbekistan Airways
Vietnam Airlines
Vueling
WindJet
XL Airways France
Yemenia

Hotels

Hilton Paris Charles de Gaulle

Roissypôle, Rue de Rome, BP16461 Tremblay En France 95708 | +33 1 49 19 77 77 | ww.hilton.com

Situated between the two terminal areas. Rooms on the fourth floor or higher offer views of the taxiways and some aprons – particularly rooms ending in 01 and 29. Windows next to the lifts also give views over the holding points. Slightly pricey.

Ibis Hotel

Roissy Aéroport Cedex BP11122 Roissy 95701 | +33 1 49 19 19 21 | www.ibishotel.com

A more affordable option is the large Ibis hotel. North facing rooms have views over Terminal 2 and northern runways, and south facing have views over Terminal 1 and the charter terminal. The hotel is also located next to the Mount spotting location.

Pullman Paris CDG Airport Hotel

Zone Centrale Ouest, BP20248 Roissy 95713 | +33 1 49 19 29 29 | www.sofitel.com

Formely the Sofitel. Another hotel located between the terminals at Charles de Gaulle. East-facing rooms have views of the taxiways and most movements. Hotel can be pricey, however.

Nearby Attractions

Paris Orly Airport

The second airport of Paris. See separate guide. Can be reached on the RER train directly from Charles de Gaulle.

Le Bourget Airport

Only a ten-minute drive, or 30 minute bus journey (line 350 or 351) from Charles de Gaulle, Le Bourget is an excellent diversion. It handles many of the executive jet traffic landing at Paris, and is also famous for the bi-annual Paris Air Salon. The museum on site has an interesting collection of airliners, including a Boeing 707, 747, Caravelle, Dassault Mercure and Concorde.

Musée de l'air et de l'espace

93352 Le Bourget | +33 1 49 92 70 62 | www.museeairespace.fr

Open daily except Monday from 10am to 6pm (5pm in winter). The museum is free, but tickets must be bought to enter certain aircraft.

This page has been intentionally left blank.

Paris Orly Airport, France

ORY | LFPO

Tel: +33 1 70 36 39 50
Web: www.aeroportsdeparis.fr
Passengers: 25,204,000 (2010)

Overview

Orly is the second busiest airport in both Paris and France as a whole. Whilst nearby Charles de Gaulle is larger and busier, Orly is still very much worth a visit as most of Air France's domestic network operates from here, as well as a number of long haul flights. Many other scheduled, charter and low-cost airlines use Orly which also wouldn't be seen at Charles de Gaulle.

Orly has two terminals – West and South. There is an official viewing location in the South Terminal which is adequate for viewing most movements. Many photographers choose to move to various spots around the perimeter for better results, however.

The airport is easily linked to Paris and Charles de Gaulle by the road, bus and train network.

As with Charles de Gaulle, aircraft photography here is officially banned, and it will often help your case if you have a letter with you to present to authorities. These will usually gain permission to continue.

Spotting Locations

1. South Terminal Observation Deck

The South Terminal has an outdoor observation area which can be reached from within the terminal. This is a good location for logging most of the airport's movements, and photography is possible (although mostly south-facing). The deck is free to enter, and often open as a smoking area through the night. If you find it closed, windows inside offer a similar view.

2. West Terminal

Upstairs in the West Terminal are a number of windows around the food court which allow views over the aircraft gates.

MAP

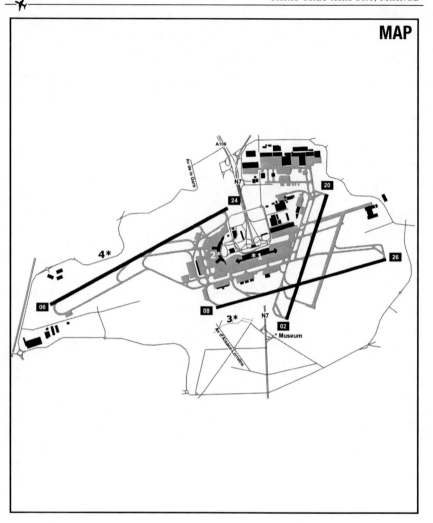

Frequencies

Tower	120.5
Pre Flight	121.05
Ground	121.7
Ground	121.825
Departure	127.75
Departure	128.375
ATIS	131.35
Approach	118.85
Approach	123.875
Approach	124.45

Runways

02/20	7,874ft / 2,400m
06/24	11,975ft / 3,650m
08/26	10,892ft / 3,320m

3. Runway 08

Take the N7 motorway underneath the airport from the South Terminal. At the first crossroads turn right. Then at the large roundabout, take the third exit – Avenue d'Alsace-Lorraine. At the end, there are places to view aircraft lining up on the runway around Rue des Mimosas. Photography is possible.

4. Runway 06

Take the A106 away from the terminals towards Paris. Leave the motorway at Rungis and head along Rue Notre Dame. Turn left at the roundabout on to Avenue de la Gare, which turns into the D167a. This eventually runs along the northern perimeter of the runway. There are places to spot and photograph aircraft around the threshold.

Airlines

Aigle Azur
Air Algerie
AirAsia X
Air Berlin
Air Burkina
Air Caraibes Atlantique
Air Europa
Air France
Air France (Air Corsica)
Air France (Airlinair)
Air France (Brit Air)
Air France (CityJet)
Air Ivoire
Air Mali
Air Malta
Air Mediterranee
Airlinair
Airlinair (Chalair Aviation)
Alitalia
Alitalia (Air One)
British Airways
Corsairfly

Cubana
easyJet
easyJet Switzerland
Europe Airpost
Flybe
Hex'Air
Iberia
Iberia (Air Nostrum)
Iran Air
Jet4you
Norwegian Air Shuttle
OpenSkies
Pegasus Airlines
Royal Air Maroc
SATA International
Syrian Air
TAP Portugal
Transavia France
Tunisair
Twin Jet
Vueling

Hotels

Ibis Paris Orly Aéroport

Orly Aerogare Cedex, BP141 Paris 94541 | +33 1 56 70 50 70 | www.ibishotel.com

A standard, affordable Ibis hotel. Even-numbered rooms on the fourth floor in particular have great views of the northern runway. Aircraft can be read off even at night. A short walk to the terminal.

Hilton Paris Orly Airport

267 Orly Aerogare Cedex, Paris 94544 | +33 1 45 12 45 12 | www.hilton.com

The pricier option at Orly, but much more comfortable. Rooms at the back of the hotel give views of the Ouest terminal and taxiway leading to Runway 25. Rooms at the front have limited views of some stands. Free shuttle operates to the terminals.

Nearby Attractions

Musee Delta Athis Paray Aviation

40 av Jean Pierre Benard, 91200 Athis Mons | +33 1 69 38 83 38 | museedelta.free.fr

A small museum on the south side of Orly Airport. In its collection is an Air France Concorde, Air Inter Dassault Mercure, a Caravelle, Mirages and various others. Open Wednesday and Saturday from 2.30-5.30pm. Entrance fee 3€ (adults), and 1€ for children aged 5 to 11 years.

Paris Charles de Gaulle Airport

(see separate entry)

Paris Le Bourget Airport

Toulouse-Blagnac Airport, France

TLS | LFBO

Tel: +33 1 70 46 74 74
Web: www.toulouse.aeroport.fr
Passengers: 6,277,386 (2009)

Overview

Although itself only a regional airport with little traffic of much note to the enthusiast, the big draw of Toulouse is the Airbus factory which churns out endless A320's, A330's, A340's and A380's destined for far corners of the globe. Many of these are unlikely to be seen again in European skies for many years, if ever, and so proves incredibly tempting for the spotter.

Regular traffic at Toulouse includes a range of domestic and European flights from Air France and other carriers, mainly by regional and medium-haul types, plus low-cost airlines. Movements are generally focussed around the rush hour periods.

Airbus traffic can be relied upon most days, with test flights of the latest aircraft off the production line operating regularly. Additionally, the recent airframes to emerge from the giant hangars can usually be seen in plentiful supply around the various aprons and maintenance areas around the airfield.

Many visitors choose to take a tour of the Airbus factory, which must be booked in advance. This gives the opportunity to see aircraft on the production line, including the massive A380. Photography is not allowed, however.

In addition to Airbus, ATR also produce their turboprop airliners at Toulouse Airport. These can also often be seen on test and delivery flights, and receiving attention on the aprons.

A small aviation museum on the western perimeter has a number of preserved airliners on display.

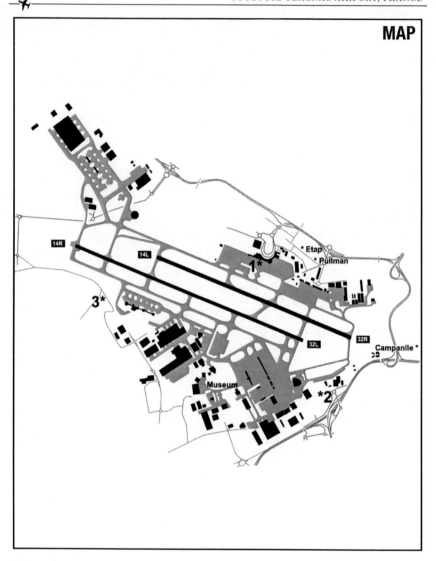

Frequencies

Ground	121.9
Clearance Delivery	121.7
ATIS	123.125
Approach	123.85
Approach	124.975
Approach	125.175
Approach	129.3
Info	121.25

Runways

14L/32R 9,843ft / 3,000m
14R/32L 11,482ft / 3,500m

Spotting Locations

1. Airport Café and Viewing Deck

Inside the terminal building is a café on the second floor. Outside is a viewing deck provided for watching aircraft, with no charge. This gives views over the runways, taxiways, gates and the distant Airbus ramps. Photography is very easy here.

2. Car Park

On the southern perimeter amongst the Airbus side of the airport is a car park from which arrivals on runways 32L/R can be logged and photographed easily, and many of the Airbus ramps can be logged. This car park is reached along the perimeter road, and by passing the Airbus car parks along Chemin de la Crabe. A short walk will yield better results.

3. Hill

A large hill exists on the western (Airbus) side of the airport which overlooks all movements on the runways, particularly in the 14L/R direction. Photography and logging are possible here. To reach the spot, head north from the terminal building. At the Pizza Hut roundabout, cross the bridge and then follow the main road alongside the runway. Turn left at the next two roundabouts, and you'll eventually reach a dirt parking area and the hill.

Airlines

Aer Lingus	easyJet
Aigle Azur	easyJet Switzerland
Air Algerie	Europe Airpost
Air Austral	Flybe
Air France	Iberia (Air Nostrum)
Air France (Air Corsica)	Jet2
Air France (Brit Air)	Jet4you
Air France (Regional)	KLM CityHopper
Air Transat	Lufthansa
Airbus Industrie	Lufthansa Regional
Alitalia	Royal Air Maroc
bmi Regional	TAP Portugal (Portugalia)
bmibaby	Tunisair
British Airways	Turkish Airlines
Brussels Airlines	Twin Jet
Eastern Airways	Vueling

Hotels

Campanile Hotel Toulouse Purpan

33 Route de Bayonne, Toulouse 31300 | +33 5 61 16 90 90 | www.campanile.fr

Although a few miles from Toulouse Airport's terminal, this affordable hotel does offer some views of aircraft on the runways, and the Airbus factory. Rooms ending in 11, 13, 17, 19, or 21 reputedly offer the best views.

Pullman Toulouse Airport

2 Avenue Didier Duarat, 31800 Blagnac | +33 5 34 56 11 11 | www.sofitel.com

Formerly the Sofitel. Rooms can be expensive, but the hotel is smart. Certain higher rooms have limited views of the terminal and remote aprons.

Etap Hotel Toulouse Airport

Avenue Didier Daurat, 31700 BLAGNAC | +33 8 92 70 12 64 | www.accorhotels.com

This hotel is located close to the passenger terminal. Odd-numbered rooms higher up facing the airport have views of all movements.

Nearby Attractions

Airbus Factory Tours

Village Aéroconstellation, Rue Frantz Joseph Strauss, 31700 Blagnac (Follow signs for Parc Aéronautique Colomiers) | +33 5 39 42 00 | www.taxiway.fr

Tours of Europe's largest aircraft manufacturing site last around 1.5 hours and take in either the A330/A340 production line, or A380 production line. You must book in advance, bring a passport, and remember that photography is not allowed inside the buildings.

Toulouse Air Museum

183 rue Gaston Doumergue, 31170 Tournefeuille | +33 5 61 70 01 | www.aatlse.org

Amongst the Airbus buildings on the western side of Toulouse Airport is a collection of historic aircraft. Amongst the airliners on display are a DC-3 and Caravelles. Another Caravelle and a Concorde production aircraft can be seen as part of the Airbus tour.

Airports in Germany

1. Cologne Bonn
2. Dusseldorf
3. Frankfurt Main
4. Hamburg Finkenwerder
5. Munich

This page has been intentionally left blank.

Cologne/Bonn Airport, Germany

CGN | EDDK
Tel: +49 22 03 4040
Web: www.airport-cgn.de
Passengers: 9,806,270 (2010)

Overview

The major draw of Cologne/Bonn for many enthusiasts is the busy UPS hub which has been based here since 1986. In addition to this, the airport is one of Germany's busiest, serving the former capital city of Bonn and a large catchment area which stretches into Luxembourg, Belgium and the Netherlands.

Cologne/Bonn was quick to embrace the low-cost revolution. Today many of the airport's flights are operated by these airlines, including foreign examples such as easyJet, Wizz Air, and home-grown airlines Germanwings and TUIfly which have bases here.

The airport has two terminals. Terminal 1 handles Lufthansa, Star Alliance and Germanwings movements, whilst all others use Terminal 2. Elsewhere, the large cargo terminal, maintenance area, and German Air Force ramp can be found between the two parallel runways.

Another note to enthusiasts is the storage area at Cologne/Bonn which has held a number of decaying aircraft for many years, as well as a few temporary resident.

Spotting Locations

1. Terminal Observation Platform

The official terrace is provided within Terminal 1 between areas B and C. These cover views over the apron and runway operations, and can usually be relied upon for logging aircraft at the cargo terminal. Photography is generally good when the windows are clean. The terrace is open daily from 6.30am to 10pm (except in poor weather) and is free.

2. Terminal 2 Car Park

The top level of the Terminal 2 Car Park is another spot with views over the passenger terminal aprons. It can also help with identifying some of the cargo aircraft, and also gives views to the stored aircraft at the far end of the airfield.

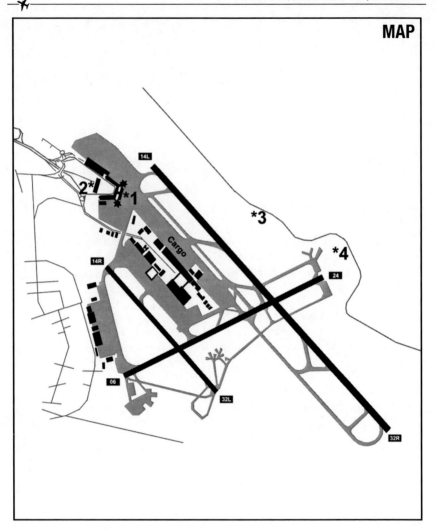

MAP

Frequencies

Apron	121.95
Ground	121.725
Director	121.05
Langen Radar	118.75
Langen Radar	126.325
ATIS	112.15
ATIS	119.025

Runways

06/24	8,068ft / 2,459m
14L/32R	12,516ft / 3,815m
14R/32L	6,112ft / 1,863m

3. Perimeter Road

For those with a car, take the road motorway leading away from the terminal, but immediately take the first exit and turn right, and right at the lights on to Alte Kölner Strasse. Follow this road for a few miles as it loosely follows the perimeter through the forest. Look for areas to park on the right. Various footpaths lead to the fence from here, giving views across Runway 14L/32R to the passenger and cargo terminals.

4. Runway 24

Following Alte Kölner Strasse a little further brings you to the end of Runway 24. There are limited places to park. This spot will give excellent photographs of aircraft on short finals for this runway.

Airlines

Air Arabia Maroc
Air Berlin
Air Europa
Air France (Airlinair)
Air Via
AtlasJet
Austrian Airlines
Austrian Arrows
bmibaby
Bulgarian Air Charter
Condor
Corendon Airlines
easyJet
EgyptAir Cargo
FedEx Express
FedEx Feeder (Air Contractors)
Freebird Airlines
Germanwings
Hamburg Airways

Iran Air
KLM CityHopper
Lufthansa
Lufthansa Regional
Lufthansa Regional (Augsburg Airways)
Pegasus Airlines
Sky Airlines
TUIfly
Turkish Airlines
Turkish Airlines (Anadolujet)
UPS Airlines
UPS Airlines (Bluebird Cargo)
UPS Airlines (Farnair Switzerland)
UPS Airlines (MNG Airlines)
UPS Airlines (Star Air)
Wind Jet
Wizz Air
XL Airways Germany

Hotels

Holiday Inn Cologne-Bonn Airport,

Waldstrasse 255, Cologne 51147 | +49 (0) 22 03 56 10 | www.holidayinn.com

Conveniently located for the airport and motorway. Rooms can be expensive at times. The hotel is not ideally suited for viewing, although some upper rooms may offer views of the passenger apron and aircraft on finals to Runway 14R.

Nearby Attractions

Dusseldorf Airport

See separate entry

Dusseldorf Airport, Germany

DUS | EDDL
Tel: +49 211 4210
Web: www.duesseldorf-international.de
Passengers: 18,988,149 (2010)

Overview

Always a popular airport because of the excellent viewing facilities and interesting mix of aircraft, Düsseldorf is also easy to get to with the current spate of low-cost airlines offering services from across Europe.

The current airport developed after the end of the Second World War, when the original was completely destroyed. Most of the current infrastructure was built between the 1950s and 1970s, however in recent years modernisation and expansion has been taking place.

The airport has a single terminal with three piers. An executive terminal is located to the west, whilst a cargo terminal and apron are to the east.

Airlines serving the airport cover a wide variety, with many of Germany's charter and leisure airlines putting in a good number of movements. A number of eastern European carriers also serve Düsseldorf, and long haul routes are offered by Delta, Emirates, Lufthansa, and Northwest Airlines

Interestingly Düsseldorf is capable of handling the Airbus A380, and is Lufthansa's first choice of diversion airport should Frankfurt be unusable. It will not feature in the airport's timetable, however.

Spotting Locations

1. Terminal Observation Deck

This terrace is located above the B pier. It allows visitors to get close to the action, with aircraft parking all around you, and the runways in the near distance. Access is via the third floor of the terminal.

2. Railway Station

The other official observation deck at Düsseldorf is at the railway station to the east of the terminal. It can be reached by the SkyTrain. Here, views of aircraft

MAP

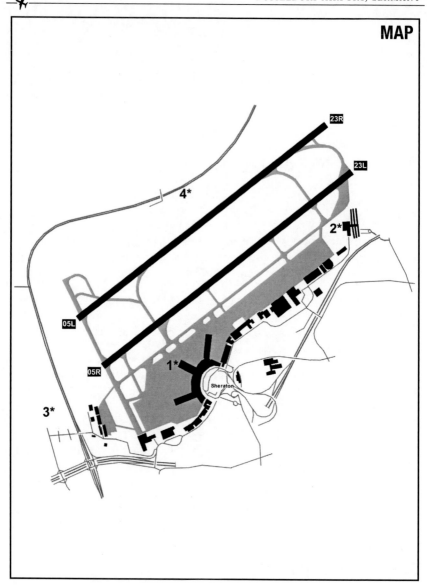

Frequencies

Ground	121.9
Clearance Delivery	121.775
ATIS	123.775
Director	119.4

Runways

05L/23R   10,809ft / 3,294m
05R/23L   10,474ft / 3,192m

using the runways can be enjoyed at close quarters, although this is only really of use when 23L/R are being used. The cargo ramp is also nearby.

Both observation areas are open daily from 6am to 9pm (8pm between 28 October and 29 March). A single ticket gives access to both areas, which costs €2 for adults, €1.50 concessions, and €1 for children. Remittance is only valid for three hours, but re-entry is welcome.

3. Liaison Village

A popular spot with locals is under the final approach path to Runway 5R in a village called Liaison. Follow Flughafenstrasse from the airport, or near the Stockum exit from the A44 Autobahn. Park the car and cross the railway tracks at the station. The path leads north under the approach path, with spectacular views.

4. Runway 5L/23R

A road runs the length of this runway, with various places to stop and get close-up shots of the action. Be careful not to obstruct emergency gates.

Airlines

Aegean Airlines	Croatia Airlines	Lufthansa
Aer Lingus	Czech Airlines	Lufthansa Regional
Aeroflot	Delta Air Lines	Lufthansa Regional
Aerosvit Airlines	easyJet	(Contact Air)
Air Berlin	easyJet Switzerland	Lufthansa Regional
Air Cairo	Emirates	(Eurowings)
Air China	Emirates SkyCargo	Mahan Air
Air France	Etihad Airways	MAT Airways
Air France (Brit Air)	Finnair	Middle East Airlines
Air France (Regional)	Flybe	Norwegian Air Shuttle
Air Malta	Germania	Nouvelair
Air Via	Germanwings	Orenair
airBaltic	German Sky Airlines	Pegasus Airlines
Al-Naser Airlines	Hahn Air	Pegasus Airlines (IZair)
AtlasJet	Hamburg Airways	Rossiya
Austrian Airlines	Iberia	Royal Air Maroc
Austrian Arrows	Iberia (Air Nostrum)	S7 Airlines
British Airways	InterSky	Scandinavian Airlines
British Airways (Sun Air)	Jat Airways	Sky Airlines
Bulgarian Air Charter	Jet2	SunExpress
Carpatair	Jet4you	SunExpress Deutschland
Condor	KLM CityHopper	Swiss European Air Lines
Corendon Airlines	LOT Polish Airlines	Swiss International

Air Lines	TUIfly	Turkish Airlines
Tailwind Airlines	Tunisair	(Anadolujet)
TAP Portugal	Turkish Airlines	XL Airways Germany

Hotels

Arabella Sheraton Airport Hotel

Im Flughafen Düsseldorf, 40474 Düsseldorf | +49 21 41 730 | www.sheraton.com

The most convenient hotel at Düsseldorf Airport, and connected to the terminal via a walkway. Rooms on higher floors with numbers ending in 10 will give views of the domestic ramp and distant taxiway. Rooms can be expensive, however.

Holiday Inn Düsseldorf Airport-Ratingen

Broichhofstrasse 3, 40880 Ratingen | +49 21 02 45 60 | www.duesseldorf-airport-holiday-inn.de

Affordable option located on the airport's eastern boundary close to the intersection of the A44 and A52 Autobahns. Views of aircraft are too distant to be of use, however users of an SBS may have more luck.

Nearby Attractions

Cologne/Bonn Airport

See separate entry

Frankfurt am Main Airport, Germany

FRA | EDDF

Tel: +49 180 5 372 4636
Web: www.frankfurt-airport.com
Passengers: 53,009,221 (2010)

Overview

Frankfurt is Germany's busiest airport, and one of the busiest in Europe. It has been a favourite with aircraft enthusiasts for many years, particularly due to the exotic mix of airliners from the all around the world.

Scheduled services began on the current airport site in 1936 after an existing airport at nearby Rebstock became overcrowded. The new Rhine-Main airport was also built as an Airship Port, and its first movements - in May 1936 - were the airships Hindenberg and Graf Zeppelin. Deutsche Lufthansa began services to the airport in July 1936 using Junkers Ju52 aircraft.

After the war the Allied forces oversaw the reconstruction of the airport, allowing commercial flights to begin again on 14 August 1946. A second parallel runway was constructed in 1949 and the airport was handed over to German control. The south side of the airport was, however, retained for military operations, a significant amount of which was by USAF aircraft.

Terminal 2 was opened in 1994, easing congestion at the original terminal complex, which now became Terminal 1 handling all Lufthansa and associated airlines. A new terminal is now in the pipeline, expected to be completed by 2015 on the site of the former air base, which vacated the site in 2005. A new, fourth, runway opened in late 2011.

As well as most of the Lufthansa and Condor fleets, Frankfurt is served by all major airlines from around the world. There are very few low-cost carriers here.

Spotting Locations

1. Terminal 2 Visitors' Terrace

The famous viewing terrace atop Terminal 1 is now long gone sadly. However, the terrace on Terminal 2 remains open. It gives close-up views of the action around this terminal, and the nearby runways and commuter ramp. It can be difficult to see movements at parts of Terminal 1 and Runway 18 from here. Opening times: daily from 10am to 6pm. Last entrance 4.30pm. Adults €5. Unfortunately it is

MAP

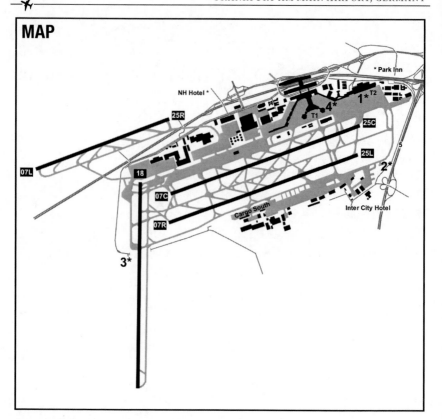

Frequencies

Tower	124.85
Tower	127.325
Apron East	121.95
Apron West	121.7
Apron South	121.85
Ground	121.8
Director	118.5
Director	124.2
Delivery	121.9
ATIS	118.025
ATIS	118.725
Info	119.15
Radar	118.45
Radar	120.15
Radar	120.8
Radar	126.55
Radar	136.125

Runways

07L/25R 9,240ft / 2,800m
07C/25C 13,123ft / 4,000m
07R/25L 13,123ft / 4,000m
18   13,123ft / 4,000m

closed from October-April, but similar views can be had from the food court inside the terminal.

2. Autobahn Bridge/Airlift Memorial

The best spot for runway 25L/C arrivals. From Terminal 2, it is possible to walk past the end of Runways 25L/C along a designated footpath. At ground level outside the terminal, follow Hugo-Eckener-Ring past the catering and office buildings. The footpath starts on the left, crossing a small bridge. Eventually the footpath rises to meet a bridge crossing the Autobahn 5. From here, excellent photographs of aircraft on short finals can be taken, and many movements logged with good binoculars. A little further on is the Berlin Airlift Memorial, with a preserved C-47 and C-54 on display.

3. Runway 18 Viewing Area

Runway 18 is north-south facing, and used primarily for departures. A viewing area and small car park was put here to cater for enthusiasts. It is good for photographing departures on Runway 18, and also aircraft on short finals for Runways 07C/R. Some aircraft on the taxiways and cargo ramps can be logged from here. Unfortunately the area has become slightly neglected recently. Some bus services pass here from Terminal 1.

4. Airside Bus Tour

It is possible to take a 45 minute bus tour of the airside facilities, including various ramps and the maintenance area (where a Vickers Viscount is kept). The tour starts at the Frankfurt Airport Centre in the bridge between terminals 1 and 2. It runs from 11am-4pm and the cost is €6.

Airlines

ACT Airlines	Air India	American Airlines
Adria Airways	Air Malta	Ariana Afghan Airlines
Aegean Airlines	Air Mauritius	Asiana Airlines
Aer Lingus	Air Moldova	Asiana Airlines Cargo
Aeroflot	Air Namibia	Atlas Air
AeroLogic	Air Transat	AtlasJet
Air Algerie	Air VIA	Austrian Airlines
Air Algerie Cargo	airBaltic	Austrian Arrows
Air Astana	AirBridgeCargo Airlines	AVE.com
Air Berlin	Albanian Airlines	Belavia
Air Canada	Alitalia	British Airways
Air China	Alitalia (Air One)	British Airways
Air France	All Nippon Airways	(BA CityFlyer)

British Airways
World Cargo
Bulgaria Air
Bulgarian Air Charter
Cargo Garuda Indonesia
Cathay Pacific
Cathay Pacific Cargo
China Airlines
China Airlines Cargo
China Eastern Airlines
China Southern
Airlines Cargo
Cirrus Airlines
Condor
Croatia Airlines
Cyprus Airways
Czech Airlines
Delta Air Lines
DHL
EgyptAir
El Al
Emirates
Emirates SkyCargo
Ethiopian Airlines
Etihad Airways
EVA Air Cargo
FedEx Express
FedEx Feeder (Air
Contractors)
Finnair
Flybe
Georgian Airways
Germanwings
Grandstar Cargo
Gulf Air
Hamburg Airways
Holidays Czech Airlines
Iberia
Icelandair
Iran Air
Iran Air Cargo
Jade Cargo International

Japan Airlines
Jat Airways
Jet4you
KLM CityHopper
Korean Air
Korean Air Cargo
Kuwait Airways
LAN Airlines
LAN Cargo
LOT Polish Airlines
LOT Polish Airlines
(EuroLOT)
Lufthansa
Lufthansa (PrivatAir)
Lufthansa Cargo
Lufthansa Regional
Lufthansa Regional
(Air Dolomiti)
Luxair
Malaysia Airlines
Malev
MASKargo
Middle East Airlines
Montenegro Airlines
National Airlines
Nightexpress
Niki
Nouvelair
Oman Air
Onur Air
Pakistan International
Airlines
Qantas
Qatar Airways
Qatar Airways Cargo
Rossiya
Royal Air Maroc
Royal Jordanian
S7 Airlines
Saravia
SATA International
Saudi Arabian Airlines

Scandinavian Airlines
Singapore Airlines
Sky Airlines
Skyways Express
Somon Air
South African Airways
Southern Air
Spanair
SriLankan Airlines
Sunny Airways
SunExpress
SunExpress Deutschland
Swiss European Air Lines
Swiss International
Air Lines
Syrianair
TACV
TAM Airlines
TAP Portugal
TAROM
Thai Airways International
TNT Airways
Transaero Airlines
TUIfly
Tunisair
Turkish Airlines
Turkish Airlines
(Anadolujet)
Turkish Airlines Cargo
Turkmenistan Airlines
Turkuaz Airlines
Ukraine International
Airlines
United Airlines
US Airways
Uzbekistan Airways
Uzbekistan Airways Cargo
Vietnam Airlines
Viking Hellas
World Airways
XL Airways Germany
Yemenia

Hotels

InterCity Hotel Frankfurt Airport

Cargo City Süd, 60549 Frankfurt | +49 69 69 70 99 | www.frankfurt-airport.intercityhotel.de

Located on the south side, close to the old USAF base. This hotel has some rooms offering limited views of the parallel runways. TV screens in the lobby often have aircraft registrations listed alongside movements. It is a short walk to the Autobahn Bridge spot.

NH Frankfurt Airport Hotel

Mörfelder Strasse 113, 65451 Frankfurt | +49 61 07 93 80 | www.nh-hotels.com

Affordable hotel, located less than 2km from the terminals, with free shuttles. It is also located a short distance from the Runway 18 spot.

Park Inn by Radisson

Amelia-Mary-Earhart-Str. 10, Gateway Gardens, 60549 Frankfurt | +49 69 90 02 760
www.parkinn.com/airporthotel-frankfurt/

This hotel is located a couple of minutes' walk from Terminal 2. Rooms on the 4th and 5th floors facing south have views of aircraft approaching runways 25L/C, and of aircraft departing 07C/R. You can also see runway 18 departures once they reach around 1,500ft.

Nearby Attractions

Technik Museum Speyer

Am Technik Museum, 67356 Speyer | +49 62 32 67 080 | www.technik-museum.de

Only an hour south of Frankfurt, the Technik Museum houses a large collection of aircraft, helicopters, cars, trains and other technical innovations. Highlights include a Lufthansa Boeing 747-200, Antonov AN-22, and DC-3. Open daily 9am to 6pm (7pm at weekends).

This page has been intentionally left blank.

Hamburg Finkenwerder Airport, Germany

XFW | EDHI

Web: www.airbus.com

Overview

Finkenwerder Airport is located in the south west of the city of Hamburg in northern Germany. It is primarily used as a manufacturing and outfitting site by Airbus, in addition to their Toulouse facility in France.

The plant is the third largest aircraft manufacturing facility in the world and employs around 10,000 staff. Airbus A318, A319 and A321 models are manufactured here, as well as sections of the A380 fuselage and wings. Some models are also brought here to have their interiors fitted and final paint schemes applied ready for delivery.

Finkenwerder doesn't have any commercial flights, but regularly handles freighters of all sizes in addition to the A300-600ST "Belugas" operated by Airbus. In addition to this, there are two daily staff flights to Toulouse, and many executive jet movements in relation to Airbus' activities.

Naturally many aircraft enthusiasts visit Finkenwerder to log new airframes, many of which will shortly be flying in far flung corners of the world and not seen again in Europe. A number of spots around the airport offer views and opportunities for photography. It is advised to park your car in one of the two lots near the delivery centre, and walk to the spotting locations. Bus line 150 from Altona station will deliver you close by if you alight at Neß-Hauptdeich.

Spotting Locations

1. Road Crossing

The most famous spot at Finkenwerder is the point where the taxiway crosses the road. Cars must stop to let aircraft cross. Standing near the dike at this point gives you close access for photographs as aircraft pass to and from the delivery centre.

2. The Dike

The dike running the length of the runway gives good views of aircraft landing and departing. It is good for photographs until late afternoon, and most aircraft parked in the open can be logged from here.

MAP

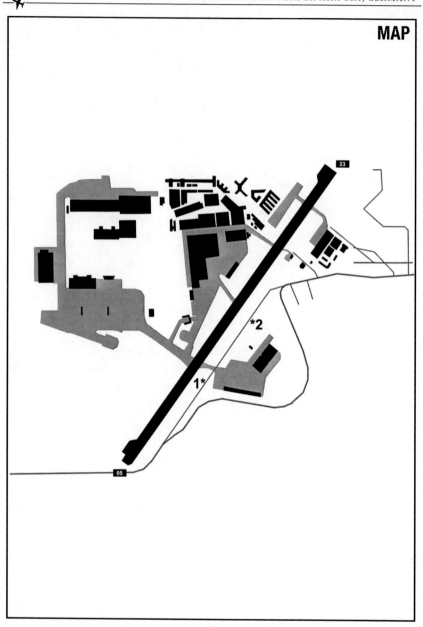

Frequencies

ATIS.................... 123.125
Info......................... 125.1

Runway
05/23   10,740ft / 3,273m

3. Delivery Centre

A new spotting area is located alongside the Airbus Delivery Centre. It gives views over the airport's ramps where you'll see plenty of new airliners being prepared for delivery.

Airlines

Germania

Hotels

Hotel Kiek-in Garni

Nordmeerstraße 48, 21129 Hamburg | +45 (0) 40 74 21 550 | www.hotel-kiek-in.de

A small and affordable hotel in a residential district very close to the delivery centre at Finkenwerder. There are no views of aircraft from the hotel, but it is very convenient.

InterCity Hotel

Paul-Nevermann-Platz 17, 22765 Hamburg | +49 (0) 40 38 0340 | www.hamburg-altona.intercityhotel.de

If you choose to stay in Hamburg itself, the InterCity is a modern and affordable option outside Altona station. This is easily accessible by car and bus from Finkenwerder, and also Hamburg's main airport.

Nearby Attractions

Hamburg Fuhlsbüttel Airport

Hamburg's main airport handles flights across German, Europe and many far away destinations. It is one of Germany's busier airports and naturally handles a lot of Germany's airlines. There are official viewing decks at each terminal and various locations around the perimeter.

This page has been intentionally left blank.

Munich Airport, Germany

MUC | EDDM

Tel: +49 89 97 500
Web: www.munich-airport.de
Passengers: 34,721,605 (2010)

Overview

Munich has in recent years become Germany's second busiest airport, and a much more important hub for Lufthansa than had been the case previously, since its Frankfurt base has become increasingly busy.

It was built to replace the old Riem airport, and opened in 1992. You will find it is a very modern airport with top-class facilities – it was even voted "Best Airport in Europe" in 2007, and has steadily risen the ranks of Europe's busiest airports. Terminal 2 was opened in 2003 to cope with the increase in traffic here, and a third runway has recently been approved for planning consultation.

As with most German airports, facilities provided for watching aircraft are of excellent quality and very popular with spotters and locals alike. The small collection of preserved historic airliners near the terminal area adds interest to visiting enthusiasts.

Spotting Locations

1. Terminal 2 Terrace

Atop Terminal 2 is a good place to log aircraft, and photography is also possible, although glass surrounds the deck. Sadly many movements at Terminal 1 are not visible from here, although aircraft can usually be seen on the runway. Terminal 2 is used by Lufthansa and its Star Alliance partners. Good binoculars are required to read off aircraft on the business ramp to the left. This location is the most popular choice, although many prefer to take a log of Terminal 1 aircraft from the Mound before moving here. Access the Terrace via the Skywalk. It is open 8am-10pm daily.

Airport Tours are available daily, which take you on a coach ride around both aprons and runways, and give you a behind-the-scenes view of various aspects of the airport. A tour lasts 50 minutes and can be booked through the airport website.

MAP

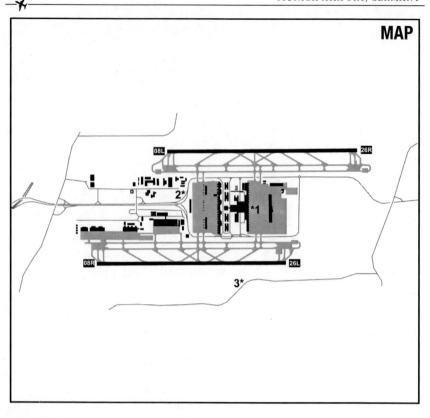

Frequencies

Tower	08R/26L 120.5
Apron	121.7
Apron	121.775
Apron	121.925
Radar	131.225
Info	120.65
Info	126.95
Ground	119.4
Ground	08L/26R 121.975
Ground	08R/26L 121.825
Director	118.825
Clearance Delivery	121.725
ATIS	123.125
Arrival	120.775
Arrival	128.025
Radar	123.9
Radar	127.95

Runways

08L/26R	13,123ft / 4,000m
08R/26L	13,123ft / 4,000m

2. Viewing Hill (The Mound)

The second official viewing location is the Mound, located between the runways close to the central terminal area. As the name suggests, this is an elevated position with views over the ramps and runways over two levels. It is open daily and has a €1 charge. Also at the spot is an aviation shop and a few preserved historic aircraft, including a DC-3, Junkers Ju-52, and Lockheed Constellation. It is possible to walk to the Mound, however the S-Bahn train service stops here one stop before the terminal.

3. Runway 8R/26L

A road runs the length of this runway, with various places to stop and get close-up shots of the action. There is also a hill at the marked location with elevated views over the runway. Be careful not to obstruct emergency gates.

Airlines

Adria Airways	British Airways	KLM
Aegean Airlines	World Cargo	KLM CityHopper
Aer Lingus	Bulgarian Air Charter	LOT Polish Airlines
Aeroflot	Carpatair	LOT POlish Airlines
Air Berlin	Cimber Sterling	(EuroLOT)
Air Canada	Condor	Lufthansa
Air China	Cirrus Airlines	Lufthansa (PrivatAir)
Air France	Croatia Airlines	Lufthansa Cargo
Air France (Regional)	Cyprus Airways	Lufthansa Regional
Air Malta	Delta Air Lines	Lufthansa Regional
Air Mauritius	DHL	(Air Dolomiti)
Air Transat	Donavia	Lufthansa Regional
Air Vallee	easyJet	(Augsburg Airways)
airBaltic	EgyptAir	Luxair
Ak Bars Aero	El Al	Niki
Alitalia	Emirates	Norwegian Air Shuttle
Alitalia (Air One)	Etihad Airways	Oman Air
All Nippon Airways	FedEx Express	Pegasus Airlines
Arkia Israel Airlines	Finnair	Pegasus Airlines (IZair)
AtlasJet	Germania	Polet Airlines
Austrian Airlines	Germanwings	Qatar Airways
Austrian Arrows	Iberia	Rossiya
BAe Systems	Iberia (Air Nostrum)	Royal Air Maroc
BinAir	Icelandair	Royal Jordanian
bmibaby	InterSky	RusLine
British Airways	Jet Air	S7 Airlines

Scandinavian Airlines	Swiss European Air Lines	Turkish Airlines
Sky Airlines	Tailwind Airlines	United Airlines
South African Airways	TAP Portugal	US Airways
Spanair	TAROM	UTair
Star Air	Thai Airways International	West Air Sweden
SunExpress	TNT Airways	Yakutia Airlines
SunExpress Deutschland	TUIfly	
Swiftair	Tunisair	

Hotels

Holiday Inn Express

Freisiner Strasse 94, Schwaig, 85445 | +49 81 22 95 880 | www.hiexpress.com

Located in the village of Schwaig, a few miles from the airport. Rooms facing the airport can be requested. If traffic is landing over you, it is very low over the hotel and easy to read off.

Hotel Kempinski

Terminalstrasse Mitte 20, 85356 Munich | +49 89 97 820 | www.kempinski-airport.de

A modern hotels in the centre of the terminal area at Munich Airport, with 389 room and suites. Slightly pricier, with rooms starting at €208, but perfect for convenience. Rooms on the upper floors have limited views of the terminal aprons.

Mövenpick Hotel Munich Airport

Ludwigstrasse 43, 85399 Munich | +49 81 18 880 | www.moevenpick-hotels.com

Located close to the end of Runway 8R. Some rooms have limited views of aircraft on final approach. The viewing locations are a short walk/drive from here.

Nearby Attractions

Deutsches Museum

Effnerstraße 18, 85764 Oberschleißheim | +49 89 21791 | www.deutsches-museum.de

Part of this museum's collection is at the Oberschleißheim Airfield to the north of the city. It incorporates the restored hangar from this historic airfield, with displays of various piston, jet and glider aircraft, plus helicopters and some aircraft restoration projects. Open daily from 9am-5pm. Basic ticket price of €6, but other options available for combining with the museum's other site in Munich.

Augsburg Airport

A small general aviation and regional airport around 35 miles west of Munich Airport. It doesn't currently have any scheduled flights, but has plenty of light aircraftm movements.

Airports in Greece

1. Athens

This page has been intentionally left blank.

Athens Eleftherios Venizelos Airport, Greece

ATH | LGAV

Tel: +30 210 353 0000
Web: www.aia.gr/
Passengers: 15,411,952 (2010)

Overview

Athens' Eleftherios Venizelos International Airport is one of Europe's newest large-scale airport facilities, and is situated to the east of the city. It was built to replace the original Hellenikon airport in the city centre, which was limited by space and unhappy neighbours.

The new airport opened in 2001, and was built with plenty of space for expansion. It features two long parallel runways and a single terminal building. It is the busiest airport in Greece, and home of Olympic Airways.

At either side of the terminal building are ramps for commuter aircraft, cargo, business and private aircraft, and maintenance.

Athens acts as a hub for flights in south eastern Europe and many carriers from surrounding countries serve the airport. Most major airlines in Europe and the Middle East serve the airport, including some low-cost carriers. Some airlines from North America and the Far East also send aircraft daily. The visitor is sure of an interesting mix on any visit.

Spotting Locations

1. McDonalds Restaurant

On the 4th floor of the terminal, this location has plenty of seating and large windows give views over the gates, taxiways and eastern runway. Photography is easy with a 200mm lens. The aspect can be a problem in winter, but is not a problem in the summer. Most movements will be seen from here.

2. Departures Level

Walking outside the terminal at Departures level, turn right and you'll find an area with views over the other runway. There are shaded seats here to enjoy the view, although photography is fairly difficult. Walking a little further to the end of the pedestrian area gives some views over the executive jet ramp.

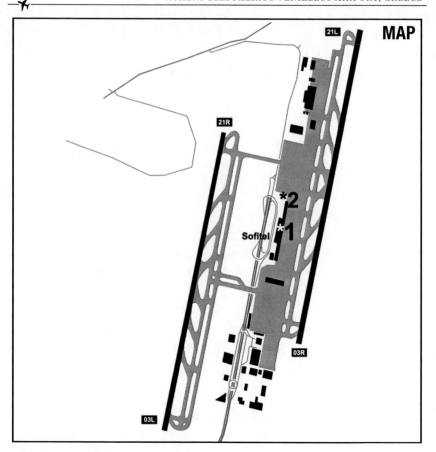

MAP

Frequencies

Tower	136.275
Info	136.025
Ground	121.75
Ground	121.8
Ground	121.9
Ground	121.95
Director	121.4
Departures	128.95
Clearance Delivery	118.675
ATIS	136.125
Arrival	126.575
Arrival	132.975
Approach	124.025
Approach	126.575
Approach	131.175

Runways

03L/21R	12,467ft / 3,800m
03R/21L	13,123ft / 4,000m

3. Perimeter Roads

Various roads lead around parts of the airport perimeter from the central road area around the terminal. These can offer various vantage points of aircraft on the runways and on short final to land depending on directions in use. Security patrols are common, however.

Airlines

Adria Airways

Aegean Airlines

Aer Lingus

Aeroflot

Aerogenesis Air Service

Aerosvit Airlines

Air Bucharest

Air Canada

Air China

Air France

Air Malta

Air Moldova

Air One

Air Transat

airBaltic

Airgo Airlines

Alitalia

Armavia

Austrian Airlines

Autrian Arrows

Belle Air

Blue1

British Airways

Brussels Airlines

Bulgaria Air

Carpatair

Cimber Sterling

Croatia Airlines

Cyprus Airways

Czech Airlines

Czech Connect Airlines

Darwin Airline

Delta Air Lines

DHL

Donbassaero

easyJet

EgyptAir

El Al

Emirates

Etihad Airways

FedEx Express

Fly Hellas

Georgian Airways

Germanwings

Gulf Air

Hellenic Imperial Airways

Iberia

Jat Airways

Jetairfly

KLM

Kuban Airlines

LOT Polish Airlines

Lufthansa

Lufthansa Cargo

Malev

Middle East Airlines

Norwegian Air Shuttle

Olmypic Air

Pegasus Airlines (IZair)

Qatar Airways

Rossiya

Royal Jordanian

Royal Jordanian Cargo

Scandinavian Airlines

Singapore Airlines

Sky Express

Sky Wings
Star Air
Swiss International Air Lines
Syrian Air
TAP Portugal
TAROM
Thai Airways International
TNT Airways
Transavia

Turkish Airlines
Tunisair
UM Airlines
United Airlines
UPS Airlines
US Airways
Vueling
Viking Hellas Airlines

Hotels

Sofitel Athens Airport

Athens International Airport, 19019 Spata | +30 21 03 54 40 00 | www.sofitel.com/athens

Situated at the airport complex, very close to the terminal. A smart and modern hotel, like the airport itself, with fantastic service. Higher rooms have views of the movements which can be read off with binoculars. Fairly expensive, though booking in advance will mean cheaper rates.

Nearby Attractions

Hellenikon Airport

The former Athens airport has been largely redeveloped since its closure in 2001. There are, however, a group of stored airliners here formerly operated by Olympic Airlines, including a Boeing 727-200, 737-200, 747-200, and a BAC 1-11. Rumour is that the site and aircraft will be used for an aviation museum in the future. You can find Hellenikon close to the city centre

Airports in Hungary

1. Budapest

This page has been intentionally left blank.

Budapest Liszt Ferenc International Airport, Hungary

BUD | LHBP

Tel: +361 296 7000
Web: www.bud.hu
Passengers: 8,190,089 (2010)

Overview

Budapest Airport is the busiest in Hungary and the home base of Malev Hungarian Airlines. What was once a Soviet hub behind the Iron Curtain. Today it is a modern European airport with a mix of low cost and traditional airlines, and a route network across Europe and further afield.

Terminal 1 is the original terminal, and today it is used for low cost carriers. On the ramps either side, cargo and military aircraft park up. Terminal 2, between the two runways, is very modern and is used by Malev and other carriers.

The airport is friendly to spotters. It also has a popular aviation museum next to Terminal 2. Keep an eye out also for the Tupolev TU-154 and Boeing 737-200 used by the fire service, partially visible behind the iconic control tower.

Spotting Locations

1. Terminal 1 Observation Deck

Atop the low-cost (original) terminal is an outdoor viewing area. It has a glass fence around, so photography can be a problem, but you'll see all movements around this terminal and runway 13R/31L. You also have distant views of Terminal 2 and the other runway. Open 6am-10pm, free admission.

2. Terminal 2 Observation Deck A

On the northern side of Terminal 2, accessed via the drop-off area, this outdoor deck has views over the northern stands and runway 13L/31R. It is open from sunrise to sunset and has an admission fee. It is better in the mornings due to the sun position. Please note - this spot has been closed due to terminal expansion work and may not reopen.

MAP

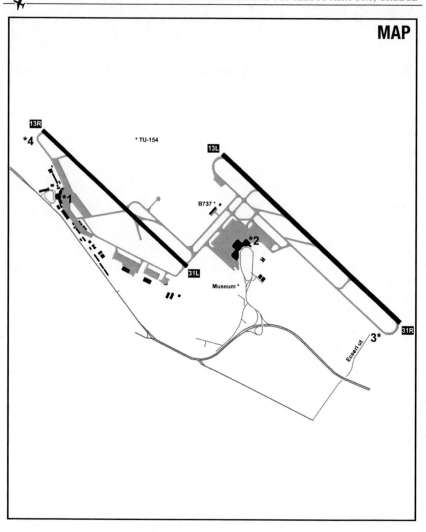

Frequencies

Ground	121.9
ATIS	117.3
ATIS	132.375
Director	119.5
Approach	122.975
Approach	129.7

Runways

13L/31R   12,162ft / 3,707m
13R/31L   9,875ft / 3,010m

3. Spotter Hill

An official spot, located down by the side of runway 31R. The spotter hill is popular with locals. You'll need a car to get here as it's a long walk from the terminal. You will be able to photograph aircraft landing and lining up. You can see some traffic using the other runway, but at a distance. To get to this spot, head to Vecses (the small town nearby), then take road Ecseri ut, go under the motorway and park at the barrier. Then walk towards the hill.

4. Cargo Hill

Close to Terminal 1 and alongside the threshold of runway 13R is the cargo hill. It is built as a noise barrier, but spotters climb up to the top and get elevated views over the runway and cargo apron. You can take excellent shots here on an afternoon. This is one of the main arrival runways.

Airlines

ABC Air Hungary	Finnair
Aer Lingus	Freebird Airlines
Aeroflot	Germanwings
Aerosvit Airlines	Hainan Airlines
airBaltic	Hi Fly
Air France	Icelandair Cargo
Air Malta	Jet2
Alitalia (Air One)	KLM
American Airlines	LOT Polish Airlines
Austrian Arrows	Lufthansa
British Airways	Lufthansa Regional
Brussels Airlines	Lufthansa Regional (Augsburg Airways)
Cargolux	Lufthansa Regional (Eurowings)
Carpatair	Malev
Cathay Pacific Cargo	Moldovian Airlines
Czech Airlines	Norwegian Air Shuttle
Delta Air Lines	Qatar Airways
DHL Aviation	Sky Work Airlines
easyJet	Solinair
easyJet Switzerland	Swiftair
EgyptAir Express	Swiss European Air Lines
El Al	Swiss (Helvetic Airways)
Europe Airpost	Tailwind Airlines
Farnair Hungary	TAP Portugal
FedEx Feeder (Air Contractors)	TAROM

TiriacAir

TNT Airways

Travel Service

Turkish Airlines

Turkish Airlines Cargo

UPS Airlines

Wizz Air

World Airways

Hotels

Hotel Ibis Budapest Airport

Ferde u. 1-3, 1091 Budapest | +361 347 97 00 | www.ibishotel.com

The closest decent hotel to the airport, around five miles away. Rooms in the range 417-425 have distant views of departures from runway 31L.

Nearby Attractions

Airport Museum

Budapest Ferihegy Airport Terminal 2

A fantastic collection of Soviet airliners related to national airline Malev and the Hungarian Air Force. The aircraft can be seen outdoors alongside Terminal 2 at the airport, but it's worth paying the entrance fee to see them up close. They include a TU-134, TU-154 and two IL-18s.

Kozlekedesi Transport Museum

11 Varosliget korut, XIV Budapest 1146 | +361 273 38 40

A museum in central Budapest with a number of aircraft in its collection. These are mainly smaller Soviet and Hungarian types. The museum is open Tuesday-Sunday, 10am-6pm (10am-5pm in October-April).

Airports in Italy and Malta

1. Malta
2. Milan Linate
3. Milan Malpensa
4. Rome Fiumicino

This page has been intentionally left blank.

Malta Luqa Airport, Malta

MLA I LMML
Tel: +356 21249 600
Web: www.maltaairport.com
Passengers: 3,290,000 (2010)

Overview

Malta is a popular holiday island and has a fairly busy airport near the main cities of Luqa and Valletta. It is home to Air Malta and a hub for various low cost airlines. During the summer months is is busy with holiday flights from the UK in particular. At other times, you will see regular flights from Italy and North African countries.

The airport has two runways. Along the western side of the field is the cargo terminal, which uses the original terminal. Lufthansa Technik also have a new maintenance hangar here, which sees a number of aircraft come and go.

Around the airfield you will also find a number of wrecks and relics of airliners, including Boeing 720 and BAC 1-11 aircraft. Malta is safe for the spotter, with a few decent locations and a friendly local spotting community.

Spotting Locations

1. Terminal Viewing Area

On the third floor of the terminal is an official viewing area, situated near a restaurant. It is free to use, and offers great views across the parking apron and main 13/31 runway.

2. Spotters Platform

From the terminal it is possible to drive or walk to the spotters platform on the opposite side of the main runway. Simply head through the tunnel under the airport, then turn left at the roundabout on the other side. You'll soon find the raised platform on your lift which is the place where many classic photographs of aircraft at Malta are taken from. The compound on your right is home to a derelict BAC 1-11 and some other aircraft.

MAP

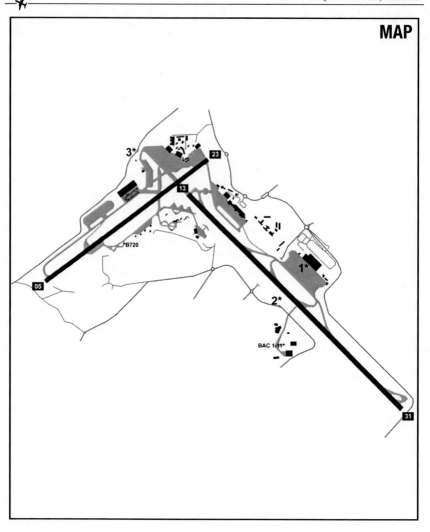

Frequencies

Tower	135.1
Apron	121.825
Apron	133.9
ATIS	127.4
Approach	118.35
Approach	128.15

Runways
05/23 7,799ft / 2,377m
13/31 11,627ft / 3,544m

3. Western Apron

The apron on the west of the field is used by overnight aircraft and also the annual air show. The road running past here has places to park, and also holes cut in the fence for spotters to use. From this spot you can see traffic using Lufthansa Technik and also GA and biz aircraft that use the smaller runway 05/23.

Airlines

Air Berlin
Air Malta
Alitalia
bmibaby
easyJet
EgyptAir Express
Emirates
Europe Airpost
Iberia (Air Nostrum)
Jettime
Libyan Airlines
Lufthansa
Luxair
Norwegian Air Shuttle
Ryanair
Scandinavian Airlines
SmartWings
Spanair
Thomas Cook Airlines
Thomson Airways
Transavia
Travel Service
TunisAir Express
Vueling

Hotels

There are no hotels in the immediate vicinity of Malta Airport.

Nearby Attractions

Malta Aviation Museum

Ta'Qali ATD 4000 | +356 21416095 | www.maltaviationmuseum.com

A nice museum situated next to the National Stadium at the former RAF Ta'Qali Aerodrome around 5 miles from Luqa Airport. The museum has a mix of wartime aircraft and airliners such as a DC-3 and BAC 1-11 cockpit section. It is open daily 9am-5pm (9am-1pm on Sundays). Admission is €5 for adults, less for concessions, and the museum is on the Blue Route of the Malta Sightseeing Bus Tour.

Hal Far Airport

Although closed in 1979, remnants of this former RAF base can be seen all around. Part of one runway is now a drag racing strip. Of note to the enthusiast are a couple of retired aircraft on site, including BAC 1-11 5N-BBQ on the north side of the drag strip. Hal Far is around 3 miles from Luqa Airport.

Milan Linate Airport, Italy

LIN | LIML

Tel: +39 02 232323
Web: www.milanolinate.eu
Passengers: 8,296,450 (2010)

Overview

The original, yet much smaller airport of Milan is Linate. It is situated much closer to the city than the larger Malpensa Airport, however it has always been limited by space and facilities. When Malpensa opened its new terminal in 2000, much of Linate's traffic moved there, leaving the facility much quieter.

Despite this, the airport is still popular with a number of international carriers from around Europe who favour bringing business passengers to the heart of the city. Some low-cost airlines and a few cargo operators also use the airport, and it is also a haven of domestic airliners which are rarely seen outside of Italy. Because of its closer proximity to the centre of Milan, Linate is also popular with business jets.

The terminal building is fairly antiquated now, but suitable for its purpose. On the opposite side of the runway is a ramp for executive and government aircraft, as well as a smaller general aviation runway.

Linate has some good opportunities for spotting, as long as precautions are taken not to rouse the suspicions of the local police or security personnel, especially with the government transport movements.

Spotting Locations

1. Terminal

Inside the terminal, the only real opportunity to spot is from the upstairs café which overlooks the apron and stands. Food is not cheap here, but it's advisable to purchase some to justify your stay. The café can be reached by following signs.

2. Perimeter Road

From the terminal, head in the direction of Milan. Shortly after passing the northern boundary, take an immediate left on to Viale dell'Aviazione. This road

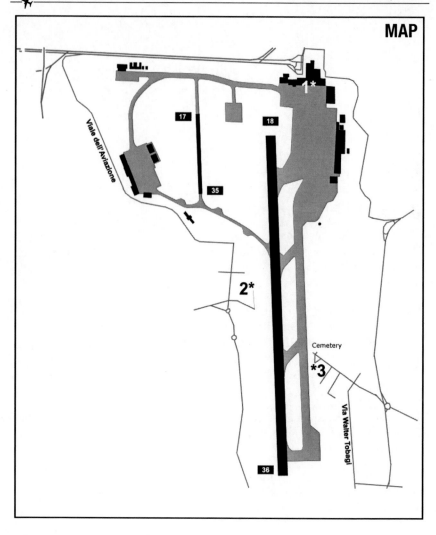

Frequencies

Tower	119.25
Ground	119.25
Ground	121.8
Departure	126.3
Departure	126.75
ATIS	125.275
ATIS	132.7
Approach	125.275
Approach	132.7

Runways

17/35 1,972ft / 601m
18/36 8,012ft / 2,442m

will lead past the military side of the airport, and eventually past a number of spots where views across the airfield can be had. Most aircraft can be read off from here with a good pair of binoculars. Following on along the road, and through the small village of Linate, the road loops around the end of Runway 36R. Various opportunities for photography can be had around this area.

3. Cemetery

One of the most popular spots around the perimeter is the cemetery. After passing the end of Runway 36, turn left on to Via Walter Tobagi and pass through the industrial estate. Eventually, turn left at the T-junction on to Via 4 Novembre and follow to the end. The car park next to the cemetery fronts the perimeter fence. Aircraft using the runway and taxiway are at extremely close quarters here. The terminal can not be seen, however.

Airlines

Aer Lingus
airBaltic
Air France
Air Malta
Alitalia
Alitalia (CityJet)
Austrian Arrows
British Airways
Brussels Airlines
easyJet

Iberia
ItAli Airlines
KLM
Lufthansa
Meridiana Fly
Scandinavian Airlines
Sky Wings
TAP Portugal
Windjet

Hotels

Holiday Inn Milan Linate Airport

Via Buozzi 2, Peschiera Borromeo 20078 | +39 (0) 255 36 01 | www.hotelcervo.it

This is a standard Holiday Inn hotel, with good facilities and clean rooms. It is one of the more affordable options for Linate, however due to its distance there are no views of aircraft movements.

Air Hotel

Via F. Baracca 2, Novegro di Segrate 20090 | +39 (0) 270 20 00 09 | www.airhotel.com

This is the closest hotel to the airport, and most convenient for travellers and visitors. The hotel is smart, but can be expensive most of the year. No views of aircraft movements.

Nearby Attractions

Malpensa Airport

Malpensa is the largest and busiest of Milan's airports, although recently Alitalia moved most of their operations to Rome. Low-cost carriers are set to increase their presence. Otherwise, airlines from around Europe, North America, and Asia fly in every day.

Bergamo Orio al Serio Airport

Milan's original low-cost airport, taken on board by Ryanair and now a lively airport in its own right. Most of Europe's low-cost airlines show up here, as well as some charter carriers. Military and stored aircraft are also in residence.

Milan Malpensa Airport, Italy

MXP | LIMC

Tel: +39 02 232323
Web: www.seamilano.eu
Passengers: 18,947,808 (2010)

Overview

The modern Malpensa airport has been an impressive airport since its revamp opened in 2000, putting the crowded old facilities behind (albeit as the secondary charter/low-cost terminal). The modern new Terminal 1 is spread over three areas, with new additions recently made. At the southern end is a cargo terminal, whilst to the north are maintenance facilities used by Alitalia. The older Terminal 2 is situated between the long parallel runways.

Alitalia unfortunately reduced its presence at Malpensa somewhat, although it does still serve a number of destinations. However, this worked in the favour of low-cost airlines such as easyJet, who increased their presence at Malpensa. It also saw Lufthansa vastly increasing their presence with the Italia brand, although this has now been reincorporated into the mainline fleet.

As with all Italian airports, the police and security presence is obvious, and spotters do not always have their approval. However, a number of spots around the airport are frequented by spotters, and give the chance to log all aircraft and photograph many.

Spotting Locations

1. Terminal 1

At the departures level in Terminal 1, large windows front the gates, aprons and distant runways. Simply walk past the rows of check-in counters. For a little more discretion, head to the right and find a hidden alcove behind the Benetton shop and play area. This offers the same view, with limited views over the cargo ramp, but is rarely patrolled by security. All movements can be seen from here; however those at Terminal 2 are harder to read off. Photography is not easy through the tinted glass.

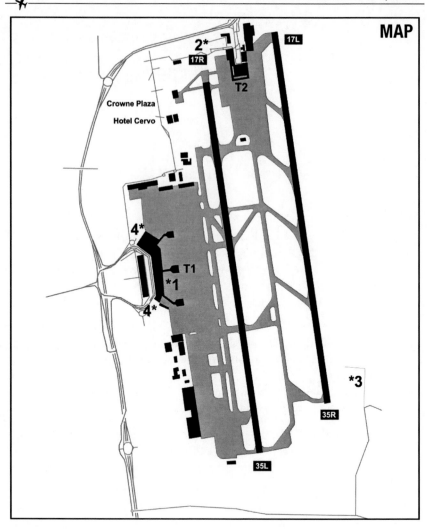

Frequencies

Tower	128.35
Ground North	121.825
Ground West	121.9
Departure	126.3
Departure	126.75
Clearance Delivery	120.9
ATIS	120.025
ATIS	121.625
Approach	125.275
Approach	132.7

Runways

17L/35R	12,861ft / 3,920m
17R/35L	12,861ft / 3,920m

2. Terminal 2

The short-stay car park outside Terminal 2 is suitable for reading off aircraft parked on one side of the terminal's apron, and also to read off aircraft using Runways 17L/R.

3. Far Side

From Terminal 1, a road named Via Strada Provincia runs south alongside the SS336 motorway, turning into Via del Gregge. Follow this to a small roundabout, and take the left exit, crossing the motorway onto Via Molinelli. Follow this road past the ends of Runways 35L/R, then turn left onto Via Case Sparse. Eventually you will reach a small car park and play area on the left. Spotters regularly congregate here. This spot is great for photographs, especially if you use the picnic benches or climbing frame! Movements on both runways can easily be read off.

4. Around Terminal 1

Walking around 500 metres in either direction from the entrance to Terminal 1 will bring you to spots where aircraft can be seen using the taxiways and nearest runway. Photography is only possible with a step or small ladder. Recent work around the Alitalia Crew Briefing Centre to the north has drastically restricted views, however.

Airlines

Aegean Airlines
Aer Lingus
Aeroflot
Aerosvit Airlines
Afriqiyah Airways
AirBridgeCargo Airlines
Air Algerie
Air Berlin
Air China
Air China Cargo
Air Europa
Air France
Air France (Regional)
Air Italy
Air Mauritius
Air Moldova
Air One
Air Seychelles
AlbaStar

Alitalia
Alitalia (Air Alps)
Alitalia (Air One)
AMC Airlines
American Airlines
Asiana Cargo
AtlasJet
Atlas Air
Austrian Airlines
Azerbaijan Airlines
Belavia
Belle Air
Biman Bangladesh
Airlines
Blu-express
Blue Air
Blue Panorama Airlines
bmi British Midland
British Airways

Brussels Airlines
Bulgaria Air
Cargoitalia
Cargolux Italia
Cathay Pacific
Cathay Pacific Cargo
China Airlines Cargo
China Cargo Airlines
China Southern
Airlines Cargo
CityLine Hungary
Cygnus Air
Cyprus Airways
Czech Airlines
Darwin Airline
Delta Air Lines
DHL Aviation
easyJet
EgyptAir

EgyptAir Cargo
El Al
ElbaFly
Emirates
Emirates SkyCargo
Estonian Air
Ethiopian Airlines
Etihad Airways
Etihad Crystal Cargo
Europe Airpost
FedEx Express
Finnair
Flybe
Germanwings
Great Wall Airlines
Gulf Air
Iberia
Icelandair
Iran Air
Israir Airlines
ItAli Airlines
Jade Cargo
Jat Airways
Jet Airways
Jet4you
KLM
Korean Air
Korean Air Cargo
LOT Polish Airlines
Lufthansa
Lufthansa Regional

Lufthansa Regional
(Air Dolomiti)
Lufthansa Regional
(Contact Air)
Lufthansa Regional
(Eurowings)
Luxair
Malev
MASkargo
Meridiana Fly
Middle East Airlines
Mistral Air
MNG Airlines
Neos
Niki
Nippon Cargo Airlines
Norwegian Air Shuttle
Nouvelair
Oman Air
Onur Air
Pakistan International
Airlines
Polet Airlines
Qatar Airways
Rossiya
Royal Air Maroc
Royal Air Maroc Cargo
Royal Jordanian
Saudi Arabian Airlines
Saudi Arabian
Airlines Cargo

Scandinavian Airlines
Silk Way Airlines
Sky Airlines
Skybridge AirOps
Singapore Airlines
Small Planet Airlines
SmaryLynx Airlines
Southern Air
SriLankan Airlines
SunExpress
Swiss International
Air Lines
Syrian Air
TACV
TAM Airlines
TAP Portugal
TAP Portugal (Portugalia)
TAROM Cargo
Thai Airways International
Transavia
Tunisair
Turkish Airlines
Turkish Airlines Cargo
Twin Jet
Ukraine International
Airlines
United Airlines
Uzbekistan Airways
Vueling
Wind Jet
World Airways

Hotels

Hotel Cervo

Via de Pinedo 1, Somma Lombardo 21019 | +39 (0) 331 23 08 21 | www.hotelcervo.it

An affordable hotel only minutes from Terminal 1. Offers shuttle service from the airport. No rooms have views of aircraft movements, but this is regarded as the most convenient hotel for spotters.

Crowne Plaza

Via Ferrarin 7 Case Nuove, Somma Lombardo 21019 | +39 (0) 33 12 11 61 | www.crowneplaza.com

Located between both terminals, with transfers available to either. Pricier option for staying at the airport, but convenient nevertheless. Views of aircraft movements are not possible.

Nearby Attractions

Linate Airport

See separate entry

Bergamo Orio al Serio Airport

Milan's original low-cost airport, taken on board by Ryanair and now a lively airport in its own right. Most of Europe's low-cost airlines show up here, as well as some charter carriers. Military and stored aircraft are also in residence.

This page has been intentionally left blank.

Rome Fiumicino Airport, Italy

FCO | LIRF

Tel: +39 06 6595 1
Web: www.adr.it
Passengers: 36,300,000 (2010)

Overview

The main airport in the Italy's capital handles a large amount of international and domestic traffic, and is one of Europe's busiest. It is situated close to the coast where the original Roman port was located, and 35km from Rome itself.

Changes in Alitalia's operations at Milan Malpensa, particularly with regard to long-haul operations, has meant an increase in the airline's presence at Rome. This has benefitted the enthusiast here. Much of the long-haul fleet will pass through over a 48 hour period, and many of the airline's European and domestic fleets will pass through regularly. The domestic MD-80 fleet are still to be found here on shuttle flights to other Italian airports, however the airline's alliance with Air One has seen more Airbus jets used.

Most of the major European carriers pass through Rome incluing a number of low-cost airlines. Long-haul flights are provided from Asia, Africa, the Middle East and North America by the usual large carriers on a daily basis. The airport is served by Emirates' Airbus A380 daily.

For the enthusiast, a good road system hugs the perimeter of most of the airport giving views of most movements. Additionally, some locations in and around the terminal buildings offer glimpses of aircraft on the ground and opportunities for photography. As always, be aware that security personnel rarely look favourably on this pastime in Italy.

Spotting Locations

1. Terminal Cafe

Upstairs in Terminal B is a café known as the Terrazza Roma Gallerie. Large windows here overlook the aprons and two of the three runways. Most movements can be seen from here. Purchasing food and showing restraint when security personnel are around is a must.

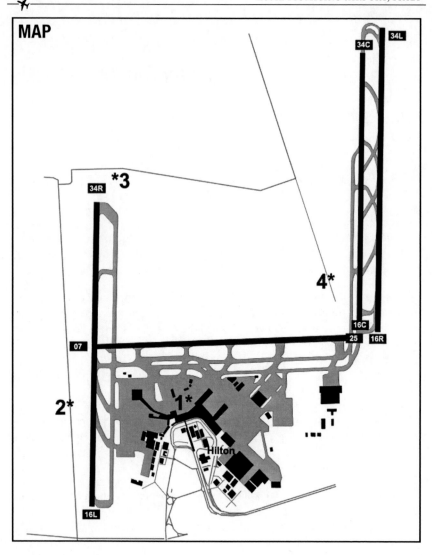

MAP

34L
34C
*3
34R
4*
16C
25
16R
07
2*
1*
Hilton
16L

Frequencies

Tower 127.625
Ground 121.8
Ground 121.9
Ground 122.125
Ramp 121.725
ATIS 114.9
ATIS 121.85
Director Arrival 119.2

Runways

07/25   10,785ft / 3,288m
16L/34R   12,740ft / 3,880m
16C/34C 11,761ft / 3,580m
16R/34L   13,163ft / 4,012m

2. Runway 16L/34R Road

Running the length of this runway is a road with many points along both sides where it's possibly to pull in and view aircraft. Photography is not really possible unless an aircraft has just lifted off. Be careful of traffic, and beware of police patrols. To reach this road, leave the terminal area in the direction of Fiumicino. You will soon pass the end of 34R and turn parallel to its length.

3. Runway 34R

Following the perimeter road from location 2, at the 34R end of the runway the road will bear right around a waterway. Around here are a number of places to pull in and watch aircraft passing overhead on short finals to the runway. Excellent for photography.

4. Between Runways

Following the perimeter road from the previous two locations, when you reach a T-junction, turn right. A number of spots here give views of aircraft on Runway 06L/24R. Continuing along the path will give you views of aircraft using Runway 25, and also across to the maintenance ramps. Beware this road leads to private properties, and is patrolled.

Airlines

Aegean Airlines	airBaltic	Cathay Pacific
Aer Lingus	Alitalia	China Airlines
Aeroflot	Alitalia (Air Alps)	China Eastern Airlines
Aerolineas Argentinas	American Airlines	Cimber Sterling
Afriqiyah Airways	Arkia Israel Airlines	Croatia Airlines
Air Algerie	Armavia	Cyprus Airways
Air Alps	AtlasJet	Darwin Airline
Air Berlin	Austrian Airlines	Delta Air Lines
Air Canada	Baboo	Eagles Airlines
Air China	Belavia	easyJet
Air Europa	Belle Air	easyJet Switzerland
Air France	Biman Bangladesh	EgyptAir
Air France (Airlinair)	Airlines	El Al
Air France (Brit Air)	Blu-express	Emirates
Air France (Regional)	Blue Panorama Airlines	Eritrean Airlines
Air Italy	bmibaby	Ethiopian Airlines
Air Malta	British Airways	Europe Airpost
Air Moldova	Brussels Airlines	Finnair
Air Seychelles	Bulgaria Air	FlyOristano
Air Transat	Carpatair	Germanwings

Gulf Air
Iberia
Iberia (Air Nostrum)
Iran Air
Israir Airlines
Jat Airways
Jet2
Kenya Airways
KLM
Korean Air
Kuwait Airways
Libyan Airlines
LOT Polish Airlines
Lufthansa
Lufthansa Regional
(Air Dolomiti)
Luxair
Malaysia Airlines
Malev
Meridiana Fly

Middle East Airlines
Mistral Air
Montenegro Airlines
Neos
Niki
Norwegian Air Shuttle
Onur Air
Qatar Airways
Pegasus Airlines
Rossiya
Royal Air Maroc
Royal Jordanian
Saudi Arabian Airlines
Scandinavian Airlines
Singapore Airlines
Sky Work Airlines
Smart Wings
SriLankan Airlines
Sunwing Airlines
Swiss International

Air Lines
Syrian Air
TACV
TAP Portugal
TAP Portugal (Portugalia)
TAROM
Thai Airways International
Transavia
Tunisair
Turkish Airlines
Ukraine International
Airlines
United Airlines
Ural Airlines
US Airways
Uzbekistan Airways
Vueling
Wind Jet
Wizz Air

Hotels

Hilton Hotel Rome Airport

Via Arturo Ferrarin 2, Fiumicino, Rome 00054 | +39 (0) 66 52 58 | www.hilton.com

This expensive hotel is connected to the terminal building and perfect for access. Certain rooms offer limited views of the domestic terminal ramp and taxiway. Aim for high floor rooms ending in 10.

Nearby Attractions

Ciampino Airport

Rome's other airport, situated closer to the city. It is a busy military and business aviation airport, with a number of low-cost operators flying throughout the day, including Ryanair and easyJet. There are a number of stored aircraft, and government transport aircraft, and also daily cargo flights by TNT and DHL.

Airports in Netherlands

1. Amsterdam Schiphol

This page has been intentionally left blank.

Amsterdam Schiphol, Netherlands

AMS | EHAM
Tel: +31 207 940 800
Web: www.schiphol.nl
Passengers: 45,300,000 (2010)

Overview

Schiphol today is one of the world's largest and busiest airports, having cemented its place in the aviation world at an early age despite the relatively small size of the Netherlands. The low-lying country was once covered by much more water than today, and the Schiphol site is testament to that. Haarlem Lake was once a vast expanse of water used by merchant ships and ferries servicing the town of Haarlem from the middle ages up until 1848 when the decision was made to drain it. The resultant land, which was flat and around 10m below sea level was soon found to be the perfect location for a landing field following the invention of powered flight. The first aircraft landed here in August 1916.

Many phases of expansion have brought about the airport we see today, with the most recent additions including the opening of the sixth runway, and an additional pier on the single terminal for the use of the ever-present low-cost airlines. Most European airlines serve Amsterdam today, as well as the major international and cargo airlines.

Schiphol is an important venue for enthusiasts and provides facilities that allow logging and photography both atop the terminal and around its perimeter.

On the site formerly occupied by the Fokker company, many business jets and smaller types can be seen, as well as maintenance activity by KLM, although these are a little harder to log and photograph.

Spotting Locations

1. Panorama Terrace

This official terrace is located along the top of the central terminal area. Although it has been reduced in size recently because of airport expansion, it still commands good views across piers B to D and most of the runways. Aircraft that are not seen arriving can usually be seen taxiing at some point. Entrance to the terrace is free. It can be reached through the entrance hall to Schiphol Central, and is

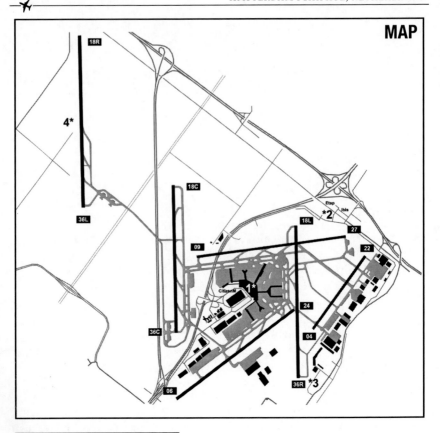

Frequencies

Tower	18C/36C	118.1
Tower	18L/36R1	19.225
Tower	18R/36L	118.275
Tower Other Runways		118.95
Approach/Departure		119.05
Approach/Departure		121.2
Approach/Departure		126.675
Arrival		118.4
Arrival		131.15
ATIS Arrival		132.975
ATIS Departure		122.2
Clearance Delivery		121.975
Clearance Delivery		121.65
Clearance Delivery		131.35
Ground NE		121.8
Ground NW		121.9
Ground SW	06/24	121.7

Runways

04/22	6,608ft / 2,014m
06/24	11,483ft / 3,500m
09/27	11,329ft / 3,453m
18L/36R	11,155ft / 3,400m
18C/36C	10,826ft / 3,300m
18R/36L	12,467ft / 3,800m

well-signposted. Facilities include an indoor cafe, restaurant and bar, and arrivals screens which usually give aircraft registrations. Opening times: from last Sunday in October 9am-5pm; from last Sunday in March 7am-8pm.

2. McDonalds

One of the official viewing areas is located alongside a McDonalds restaurant to the north of Runway 27. Most of the airport's movements can be seen here, as well as the maintenance and business jet ramps. Photography is not perfect here due to the south-facing aspect, however some aircraft are at close quarters on the runway.

3. Runway 36R

When landings are on this runway, this spot offers great photographs. In the industrial estate next to the threshold of the runway, turn right at the gas station, where there is plenty of parking space. On the afternoon, drive past the approach lights and take the second right for a spot with the sun behind you.

4. Runway 18R/36L

Two official viewing locations have been sited alongside the new sixth runway. Naturally a car or cycle is required to get there. There are spots to park, and good views of traffic arriving or departing on the runway.

Airlines

Adria Airways	Arkia Israel Airlines	China Airlines Cargo
Aer Lingus	Armavia	China Cargo Airlines
Aeroflot	Austrian Airlines	China Southern Airlines
Air Arabia Maroc	Austrian Arrows	Cimber Sterling
Air Astana	Azerbaijan Airlines	CityJet
Air Berlin	B&H Airlines	Corendon Airlines
Air Europa	Belavia	Corendon Dutch Airlines
Air France	BH Air	Croatia Airlines
Air France (CityJet)	Blue1	Cyprus Airways
Air France (Regional)	bmibaby	Czech Airlines
Air Malta	British Airways	Delta Air Lines
Air Mediterranee	British Airways	DHL
Air Transat	(BA CityFlyer)	Dutch Coast Guard
AirBaltic	Bulgaria Air	easyJet
AirBridgeCargo Airlines	Cargolux	easyJet Switzerland
Alitalia	Cathay Pacific	EgyptAir
Amsterdam Airlines	Cathay Pacific Cargo	El Al
Arkefly	China Airlines	Emirates

Emirates SkyCargo
Estonian Air
Europe Airpost
EVA Air
Finnair
Flybe
Garuda Indonesia
Great Wall Airlines
HiAir
Iberia
Icelandair
Iran Air
Israir
Jade Cargo International
Jat Airways
Jet2
Jett8 Airlines
Kalitta Air
Kenya Airways
KLM
KLM Cargo
KLM CityHopper
KLM (PrivatAir)
Korean Air
LAN Cargo
LOT Polish Airlines

Lufthansa
Lufthansa Cargo
Lufthansa Regional
Malaysia Airlines
Malev
MASKargo
MAT Airways
Nippon Cargo Airlines
Norwegian Air Shuttle
Olympic Air
Onur Air
Pakistan International
Airlines
Pegasus Airlines
Pegasus Airlines (IZair)
Rossiya
Royal Air Maroc
Royal Jordanian
Saudi Arabian
Airlines Cargo
Scandinavian Airlines
Singapore Airlines
Singapore Airlines Cargo
Sky Airlines
Sky Work Airlines
Southern Air

SunExpress
Sunwing Airlines
Surinam Airways
Swiss International
Airlines
Syrian Air
TACV
TAP Portugal
TAP Portugal (Portugalia)
TAROM
TNT Air Cargo
Transavia
Tristar Air
Tunisair
Turkish Airlines
Turkish Airlines
(Anadolujet)
Ukraine International
Airlines
United Airlines
US Airways
Viking Hellas
Volga-Dnepr
Vueling
Wind Jet
World Airways

Hotels

CitizenM Hotel

Jan plezierweg 2, 1118 BB Amsterdam Schiphol | +31 20 8117080
www.citizenmamsterdamairport.com

A modern, cheap hotel which is part of a popular chain. All rooms have double beds, and are very compact. Check-in is via a computer in the lobby, however staff can then make changes if you request them, such as a room overlooking the airport. Rooms on the 4th and 5th floor should be fine, and look out over the low-cost H pier, plus the runways and taxiways beyond. If you are lucky with the runways in use, and use SBS or an online tracker, you shouldn't miss much.

Etap Hotel

Schipholweg 185, 1171 PK BADHOEVEDORP | +31 203 483 533 | www.etaphotel.com

One of the cheapest of the hotels at Schiphol. The Etap is also conveniently located next to the McDonalds viewing location. Alternatively, the central terminal area is a five minute drive. There is a free airport shuttle for guests.

Ibis Amsterdam Airport

Schipholweg 181, 1171 PK BADHOEVEDORP | +31 205 025 100 | www.ibishotel.com

Next door to the Etap is the Ibis hotel, which offers similar convenience for spotting locations, and a free shuttle to the terminal.

Nearby Attractions

National Aviation Theme Park Aviodrome

Pelikaanweg 50, 8218 PG Lelystadt Airport | +31 900 284 6376 | www.aviodrome.nl

Located at Lelystadt Airport, 45 minutes from Schiphol. This museum has many restored historic aircraft, with particular emphasis on Dutch aviation. Most notable are the last flying DC-2 in the world, the first Fokker F27 Friendship built, flying Antonov AN-2 and Catalina, and a former KLM Boeing 747-206B (SUD). Pleasure flights are often available in the flying aircraft.

Rotterdam Airport

Rotterdam Airport is a 45 minute drive to the south. A viewing area within the terminal will give views of most of the movements, which include KLM and VLM commuter aircraft, low-cost flights by Transavia, and many business and private movements.

This page has been intentionally left blank.

Airports in Norway

1. Oslo Gardermoen

This page has been intentionally left blank.

Oslo Gardermoen Airport, Norway

OSL | ENGM

Tel: +47 915 06400
Web: www.osl.no
Passengers: 19,091,036 (2010)

Overview

Gardermoen was opened as Oslo's main airport in October 1998, when the existing Fornebu Airport was closed. It had already been operating as a military air base since the 1940s.

The airport is large and modern, with two parallel runways. It is the busiest in Norway, and the second busiest in Scandinavia. Expansion is taking place, with a third pier due to open in 2012. It is a busy hub for SAS, Norwegian Air Shuttle, and Wideroe, and is served by most European airlines, plus many from further afield.

The Norwegian Air Force maintain their base at the airport, with Lockheed Hercules aircraft stationed and their own operating area situated on the northern and western sides of the field.

There are a number of places to watch aircraft at Oslo, although the distance between the runways can make it difficult to monitor all movements.

Spotting Locations

1. SAS Museum Terrace

Alongside the SAS Museum on the western side of the airport is a specially-built spotting terrace. This is open 24 hours, free of charge and gives views over Runway 01L/19R. You can also see aircraft around the terminal area, but from a distance.

2. Spotting Mound

A short distance north of the SAS Museum along the 176 road and past the GA terminal is a mound in the forest which gives you elevated views of aircraft using Runway 01L/19R. It is perfect for landing shots, and you can see across the airfield. It is too distant from the terminal to see much, however.

MAP

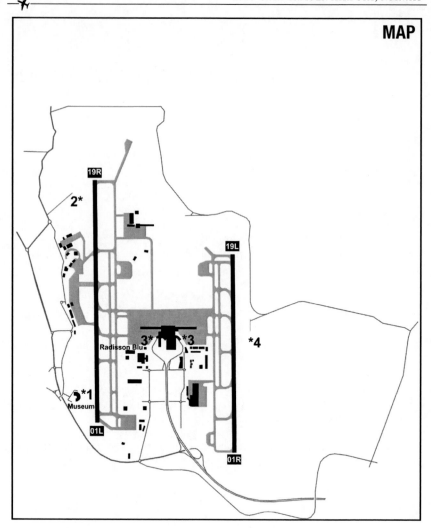

19R

2*

19L

3* *3

Radisson Blu

*4

*1
Museum

01L

01R

Frequencies

Tower	120.1
Ground	121.675
Ground	121.725
Ground	121.925
Director	131.35
Clearance Delivery	121.6
ATIS Arrival	126.125
ATIS Departure	127.15
Approach	119.975
Approach	120.45

Runways

01L/19R	11,811ft / 3,600m
01R/19L	9,678ft / 2,950m

3. Terminal Ramp

Either side of the terminal at departures level you have a view over the south side of the piers. This is perfect for logging aircraft parked there, and taking ground shots.

4. Eastern Mound

Alongside Runway 01R/19L is another mound which gives you elevated views of the runway, and across to the International Pier and SAS Hangar. Unfortunately you need to walk to this spot from the road.

Airlines

Aeroflot
airBaltic
Air Berlin
Air France
Air Mediterranee
Air Norway (North Flying)
Austrian Airlines
Austrian Arrows
Blue1
British Airways
British Airways (Sun Air)
Brussels Airlines
Cimber Sterling
Czech Airlines
Danish Air Transport
Danu Oro Transportas
Estonian Air
Finnair
Icelandair

Iceland Express
KLM
Lufthansa
Lufthansa Regional
Malmo Aviation
Norwegian Air Shuttle
Novair
Orbest Orizonia Airlines
Pakistan International Airlines
Qatar Airways
Scandinavian Airlines
SATA International
SunExpress
Swiss International Air Lines
TAP Portugal
Thai Airways International
Turkish Airlines
United Airlines
Wideroe

Hotels

Radisson Blu Airport Hotel Oslo

Hotelvegen, P.O. Box 163, N - 2061 Gardermoen | +47 63 93 30 00
www.radissonblu.com/hotel-osloairport

Quite expensive, but ideally located. Has many rooms higher up that have views of movements on runways 01L/19R. Hotel can usually accommodate your request.

Nearby Attractions

SAS Museum

OSLAT, 0080 Oslo | +47 64 81 80 05 | www.sasmuseet.net

On the western side of Gardermoen Airport, next to the GA building, is the SAS Museum. It doesn't have any aircraft on display, but has plenty of historic photographs, uniforms, models and information. It also has a useful 24 hour spotting terrace. Museum open Tuesdays (10am-3pm) and Sundays (12-4pm). Bus numbers

Sandefjord Airport, Torp

Oslo's 'low-cost' airport, situated around 70 miles south of the city. It is served by airlines such as Norwegian Air Shuttle, Ryanair, Wizz Air, Wideroe and KLM. The only place to view what's on the ground is the 'Ansatt' car park, which is in walking distance from the terminal.

Kjeller Airfield

A busy general aviation airfield to the east of Oslo. This is Norway's oldest airport, and has a small museum on site. It also hosts an airshow each May.

Airports in Poland

1. Warsaw

This page has been intentionally left blank.

Warsaw Chopin Airport, Poland

WAW | EPWA

Tel: +48 22 650 4220
Web: www.lotnisko-chopina.pl
Passengers: 8,712,384 (2010)

Overview

Poland has seen a massive boom in the number of flights to its airports with the advent of low-cost carriers such as Ryanair and Wizz Air. By far the largest and busiest airport in the country is at the capital, Warsaw.

In addition to the low-cost airlines, national carrier LOT still plies its trade to many European destinations, and other European carriers make daily visits to the airport. Sadly the days of Russian airliners are now long gone, however you will see the Polish Government's various Russian aircraft here.

Unfortunately the airport's viewing deck is now closed, but there are various other opportunities for logging aircraft at the airport. If you are travelling through the airport, there are plenty of views once airside.

Spotting Locations

1. Terminal Extension

Inside the newer part of the terminal you have views of aircraft on parts of the passenger ramp, as well as those on the military and government ramp. You can easily read them off.

2. Bus Terminus

The most popular spot now that the balcony has closed is the Bus Terminus outside the terminal. Although you can't see many of the stands from here, you will see most aircraft movements if you hang around long enough.

MAP

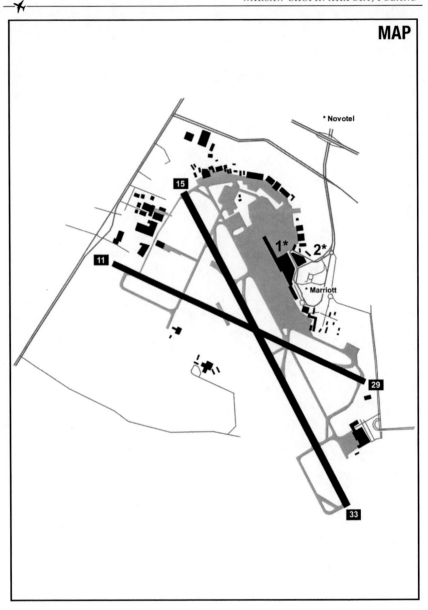

Frequencies

Ground	121.9
Delivery	121.6
Approach	125.050
Departure	128.8

Runways

11/29	9,186ft / 2,800m
15/33	12,106ft / 3,690m

Airlines

Adria Airways
Aer Lingus
Aeroflot
Aerosvit Airlines
Aerosvit Airlines (Dniproavia)
airBaltic
Air France
Air Poland
Alitalia
AMC Airlines
Austrian Arrows
Belavia
BH Air
British Airways
Brussels Airlines
Bulgarian Air Charter
Czech Airlines
DHL Aviation
El Al
Enter Air
FedEx Express
Finnair
Genex
Iceland Express (Astraeus Airlines)
Jet4You
KLM
KLM CityHopper

LOT Polish Airlines
LOT (EuroLOT)
LOT Charters
Lufthansa
Lufthansa Regional
Lufthansa Regional (Augsburg Airways)
Lufthansa Regional (Eurowings)
Malev
Norwegian Air Shuttle
Nouvelair
OLT Jetair
Royal Air Maroc
Royal Wings
Scandinavian Airlines
Sky Airlines
Small Planet Airlines
SprintAir
Swiss International Air Lines (Contact Air)
TAP Portugal
TNT Airways
Travel Service
Turkish Airlines
Ukraine International Airlines
UPS Airlines
Vueling
Wizz Air
YES Airways

Hotels

Courtyard by Marriott

1 Zwirki i Wigury Street, Warsaw, 00906 | +48 22 650 01 00 | www.marriott.com

The closest hotel to the passenger terminal. Some rooms may have very limited views of aircraft on the terminal ramps.

Novotel Warsaw Airport

UL. 1 Sierpnia 1, 02-134 Warsaw | +48 22 575 60 00 | www.novotel.com

An affordable hotel close to the airport. There are no known views of movements, however.

Nearby Attractions

Wojska Polskiego Museum

Aleje Jerozolimski 12, 00-495 Warszawa | +48 22 629 52 71 | www.muzeumwp.pl

A military vehicle museum in Warsaw with a number of aircraft, weapons and tanks on display. Aircraft include some fighters, helicopters and an An-26 transport. The museum is open Wednesday-Sunday from 10am-4pm (Closes 5pm on Wednesdays, when admission is also free).

Modlin Airport

This is a new airport on a former military airfield some 20 miles from Warsaw. A new terminal is being constructed ahead of the 2012 UEFA football championships, and will be served by low cost airlines.

Airports in Portugal

1. Faro
2. Lisbon

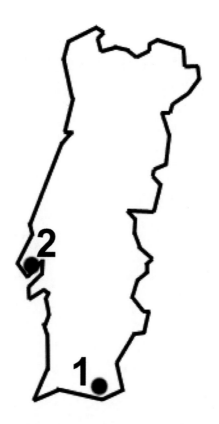

This page has been intentionally left blank.

Faro Algarve Airport, Portugal

FAO I LPFR

Tel: +351 289 800 617
Web: www.ana.pt
Passengers: 5,447,200 (2010)

Overview

Serving the popular Algarve region on Portugal's south coast, Faro is a busy holiday airport served primarily by European charter and low-cost operators. It is also served by a number of scheduled operators

Faro has a single terminal building, and a single runway. There are no official viewing locations, but photographers will love the opportunities alongside the runway, especially given the year-round sun is always behind you. Naturally Faro is busier in the summer months.

Spotting Locations

1. Runway 28

A track runs the length of the runway on its south side. However, one of the better spots on this track is close to the end of Runway 28. From here you can easily see and photograph arrivals and departures. To reach the spot, drive past the fire station and park. You then need to walk towards and alongside the fence until an elevated area gives you the best views.

2. Runway 10

Again, whilst a track runs along the length of the runway and you can find a spot to suit, one of the better locations is at the end of Runway 10. A road runs past the end of the runway, and shortly afterwards a track on the left turns towards the runway. You can park along here and walk to find the best spot for you. A stepladder may be needed for photographs.

MAP

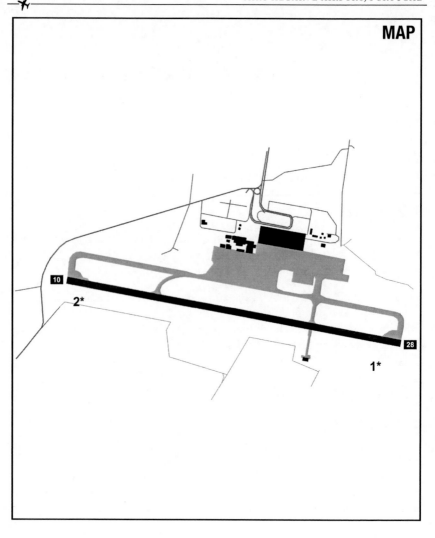

Frequencies

Ground................118.575
ATIS......................124.2
Approach...............119.4

Runways
10/28   8,169ft / 2,490m

Airlines

Aer Lingus

Air Berlin

Air Transat

Arkefly

Austrian Airlines

bmibaby

British Airways

British Airways (BA CityFlyer)

Brussels Airlines

easyJet

easyJet Switzerland

Edelweiss Air

Europe Airpost

Flybe

Germanwings

Holidays Czech Airlines

Jetairfly

Jet2

Lufthansa

Luxair

Monarch

Niki

Norwegian Air Shuttle

Orbest Orizonia Airlines

Ryanair

SATA Air Acores

TAP Portugal

Thomas Cook Airlines

Thomas Cook Airlines Belgium

Thomson Airways

Transaero

Transavia

TUIfly

TUIfly Nordic

Hotels

There are no hotels in the immediate vicinity of Faro Airport.

Nearby Attractions

Airfields

There are a number of small general aviation, skydive and microlight airfields along the Algarve coast. The most notable include Portimao and Lagos, around 35 and 40 miles west of Faro respectively.

This page has been intentionally left blank.

Lisbon Portela Airport, Portugal

LIS | LPPT

Tel: +351 218 413 700
Web: www.ana.pt
Passengers: 14,035,273 (2010)

Overview

Although one of Europe's quietest capitals, a trip to Lisbon can still yield a number of exotic aircraft, and the opportunity to spot in the sun is never to be scoffed at.

Flying directly to Lisbon is an option with most European airlines, and a number of long haul carriers from North and South America, and Africa (such as TAAG Angola). Alternatively, the drive from the Algarve is less than three hours.

The Portuguese Government finally announced in 2011 that it has decided to abandon plans to build a replacement airport at Alcochete, to the north of the city, on the site of the current military airfield there. So the current airport, which is hemmed in by motorways and buildings, will struggle to cope with current movements and passenger numbers.

Lisbon is the main operating base of Portuguese national carrier TAP, as well as PGA Portugalia, Sata International, and EuroAtlantic. A number of low-fare carriers now operate into Lisbon. It has recently opened the modern Terminal 2.

Spotting Locations

1. Calvanas

This is the most popular spot to watch and photograph aircraft at Lisbon. It includes a small hill overlooking the threshold of Runway 03, with unobstructed views and perfect sunlight all afternoon. It is not really suitable when the Runway 21 direction is in use. To drive there, take the Camarate/Charneca/Alvalade exit from the south/westbound E01 motorway, then take the first right and find somewhere to park near the houses. Alternatively Bus 17 will drop you at Calvanas if you ask the driver. There are snack bars close by.

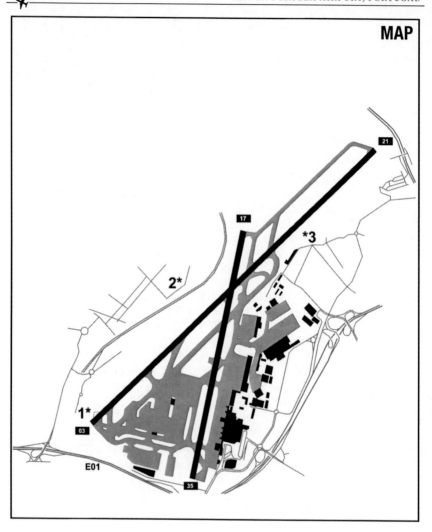

Frequencies

Tower	118.95
Radar	127.9
Info	123.75
Info	124.35
Info	131.05
Ground	121.75
Clearance Delivery	118.95
ATIS	124.15
Approach	119.1

Runways

03/21	12,484ft / 3,805m
17/35	7,559ft / 2,304m

2. Runway 03/21

Half-way along Runway 03/21 is another spot which can offer good photography, and an overview of all the airport's movements, and aircraft parked on the various ramps. To reach the spot, follow directions to location 1, but continue along the road after leaving the motorway at Camarate/Charneca/Alvalade. Take the 2nd exit at the roundabout and continue.

3. Raised Area

Walking from the terminal along the approach road, you will come to a busy roundabout. Take the first exit on the left and follow the footpath up the hill, with a small football pitch nearby. From here, aircraft using the runway and taxiways can be observed, and aircraft on the remote stands can be logged. It is unfortunately not a great spot for photography.

Airlines

Aer Lingus	Orbest
Aero VIP	Onur Air
Aigle Azur	Royal Air Maroc
Air Europa	Royal Air Maroc Express
Air France	SATA International
Air France (Regional)	Star Air
Air Moldova	STP Airways (euroAtlantic Airways)
Air Transat	Sun d'Or (El Al)
Blue Air	Sunwing Airlines
bmibaby	Swifair
British Airways	Swiss International Air Lines
Brussels Airlines	TAAG Angola Airlines
DHL	TACV
Dubrovnik Airline	TAP Portugal
easyJet	TAP Portugal (Portugalia)
easyJet Switzerland	TAP Portgual (White)
FedEx Express	TNT Airways
Finnair	Transaero
Flyant	Transavia
Germanwings	Tunisair
Iberia	Turkish Airlines
Iberia (Air Nostrum)	Ukraine International Airlines
KLM	United Airlines
LAM Mozambique (euroAtlantic Airways)	UPS Airlines
Lufthansa	US Airways
Lufthansa Regional (Eurowings)	Vueling
Niki	White

Hotels

Radisson SAS Lisbon Airport

390 Avenue Marechal Craveiro Lopes, Lisbon 1749-009 | +351 (21) 004 5000
www.lisbon.radissonsas.com

The only hotel at Lisbon with any aircraft views. Even-numbered rooms on the 10th floor yield the best results. This hotel is fairly expensive.

Nearby Attractions

Montijo Naval Air Base

An airfield across the bay from Lisbon Airport. Home to some naval transport aircraft. You can see aircraft approaching and departing, but there are no good areas to see what is on the ground.

Sintra Air Base/Aircraft Museum

+351 21 958 27 82 | www.emfa.pt/www/po/musar/

This is a military training facility to the north west of Lisbon, and also home to the Sintra Aircraft Museum. If you let the guards know that you're visiting the museum, you will be allowed in and can log aircraft parked on the ground. The museum has 20 aircraft, and is open daily except Monday.

Airports in Spain and Canary Islands

1. Alicante
2. Barcelona
3. Madrid Barajas
4. Malaga
5. Palma de Mallorca
6. Tenerife South

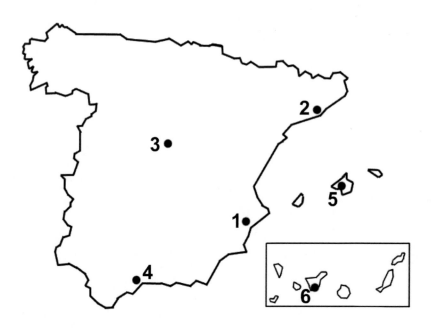

This page has been intentionally left blank.

Alicante Airport, Spain

ALC | LEAL

Tel: +34 91 321 10 00
Web: www.aena-aeropuertos.es
Passengers: 9,382,935 (2010)

Overview

Alicante is one of Spain's busiest airports, and a popular holiday destination serving the tourist resorts along this part of the coast. The airport is also one of Ryanair's biggest bases, with most passengers travelling on the airline's flights from all over Europe.

Recently a new terminal opened, replacing the existing terminals 1 and 2, which are currently closed and likely to be demolished soon. Despite how busy it has become, Alicante only has one runway.

Although no official viewing areas are provided, Alicante is quite popular among enthusiasts with a variety of unofficial locations which are perfect for logging and photographing movements. It is best to have the use of a car when spotting at Alicante.

Spotting Locations

1. Terminal Area

If you walk from the terminal to the west and head for the fence, you will be able to see GA and cargo aircraft, and there are some opportunities for quick photos. Don't loiter too long here as security will likely approach you.

2. South Side of Runway

The best spot to get a good overview of all movements, and have opportunities of photographing aircraft on the runway. To reach this spot from the terminal, head along the local road towards Elche, then turn left at the next roundabout onto CV849. Eventually you'll see a gravel track on the left running alongside the perimeter fence. You can park here and use the mound to get elevated views.

MAP

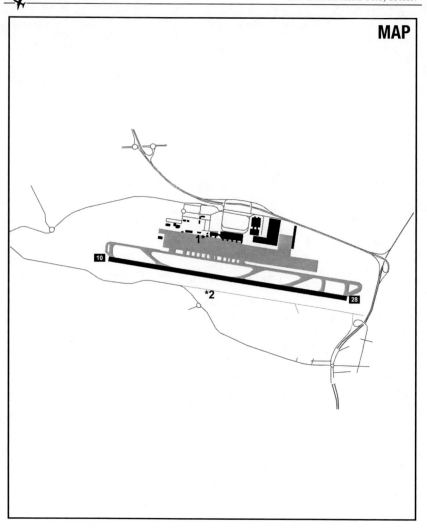

Frequencies

Tower	118.15
Tower	119.075
Ground	121.7
ATIS	113.8
Approach	118.8
Approach	120.4

Runways

10/28   9,842ft / 3,000m

Airlines

Aer Lingus
Air Algerie
Air Europa
Air Finland
bmibaby
Cimber Sterling
DHL
easyJet
easyJet Switzerland
Flybe
Goodfly
Iberia
Iberia (Air Nostrum)
Iceland Express
Icelandair
Jet2
Jetairfly
Monarch
Nordwind Airlines
Norwegian Air Shuttle
Orbest Orizonia Airlines
Ryanair
Scandinavian Airlines
Spanair
S7 Airlines
Thomas Cook Airlines
Thomas Cook Airlines Belgium
Thomson Airways
Transaero
Transavia
Tunisair
VIM Airlines
Vueling
Wizz Air

Hotels

There are no hotels at Alicante Airport which offer any views of movements.

Nearby Attractions

Murcia San Javier Airport

Situated around 35 miles south of Alicante Airport, this is a medium sized airport which doubles up as an air base and handles around 1.5 million passengers per year. Passenger operations mainly focus on Ryanair, easyJet, bmibaby and Jet2 and various charter airlines.

Valencia Airport

A fairly large airport handling close to 5 million passengers in 2010. It hosts flights from many European airlines, and is the home of Iberia partner Air Nostrum. This is primarily a scheduled airport, with holiday flights using other airports along the coast. A motorway bridge next to the Repsol petrol station is a good place to watch and photograph arrivals. Valencia is around 90 miles north of Alicante.

Barcelona El Prat Airport, Spain

BCN | LEBL

Tel: +34 91 321 1000
Web: www.aena-aeropuertos.es
Passengers: 29,209,595 (2010)

Overview

Barcelona is Spain's second city, and since the Olympic Games of 1992 has had an airport to match this status. It is located 10km from the city centre in the area of El Prat, and opened on the site in 1918.

Despite living in the shadow of Madrid Barajas, Barcelona has held its own with an extensive network of domestic, intra-European, and long-haul flights by a number of carriers. The main Spanish carriers all have a strong presence here, as do Europe's low-cost airlines. In addition to this, Barcelona is served by a number of long-haul airlines – particularly to North and South America. Singapore Airlines is the main operator to Asia.

A new terminal opened between the two parallel runways in 2009 which has greatly relieved pressure on the airport and allowed further expansion.

Spotting Locations

1. Runway 20

From Terminal 1, follow the main road out and take the first exit. Turn right on to Ronda del Sud and follow until you reach a roundabout. Go straight over, then go right at the next roundabout. At the next roundabout, find somewhere to park. This spot is not too bad for photography.

2. Spotting Tower

From the first location, continue along Carretera de l'Aviación. Turn right at the first roundabout, and go straight over the next one. You will soon come to the approach lights for Runway 25R. Here, there are benches and some shade. Aircraft are at close quarters as they approach this runway. Plenty of people congregate here, and cyclists pass regularly. An elevated viewing platform was constructed in 2009, allowing you views over the fence line and good photography opportunities.

MAP

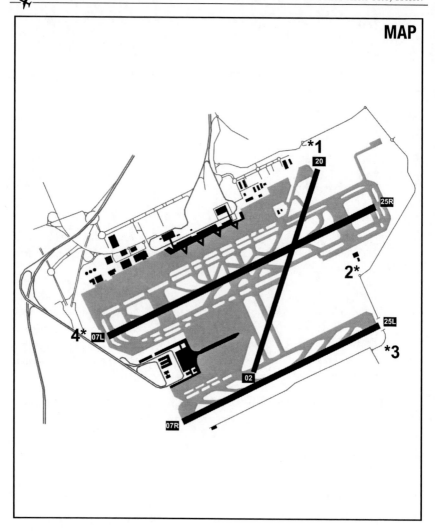

Frequencies

Tower	118.325
Clearance Delivery	121.8
ATIS Arrival	118.65
ATIS Departure	121.975
Approach	118.05
Approach	119.1
Approach	124.7
Approach	125.25
Approach	126.5
Approach	127.7

Runways

02/20	8,293ft / 2,528m
07L/25R	10,997ft / 3,352m
07R/25L	8,727ft / 2,660m

3. Runway 25L

Follow the road from the Spotting Tower location until you reach the end of Runway 25L. Again, there are places to park. Aircraft approaching the runway are very close to you and fine for photographs. A ladder is needed for good shots over the fence.

4. Runway 07L

When the 07 direction is in use, this spot offers the best chances of photography. From the terminal, follow the main road and take the first exit, heading south on the C-31 in the direction of Castelldefels. Take the first exit from this motorway, and soon you will see aircraft approaching the runway. Take the exit on to Carretera de l'Accés al Camping, and park on the rough ground immediately.

Airlines

Adria Airways
Aegean Airlines
Aer Lingus
Aeroflot
Aerolineas Argentinas
Aeromexico
Air Algerie
Air Arabia Maroc
AirBaltic
Air Berlin
Air Canada
Air Europa
Air France
Air France (Brit Air)
Air France (Regional)
Air Transat
Air Vallee
Alitalia
American Airlines
Armavia
Astra Airlines
Arkefly
Arkia Israel Airlines
Austrian Airlines
Austrian Airlines
(Lauda Air)
Avianca

Belle Air
Blue Air
bmibaby
British Airways
British Airways
(BA CityFlyer)
British Airways
World Cargo
Brussels Airlines
Cargolux
Cimber Sterling
City Airline
Croatia Airlines
Delta Air Lines
DHL
easyJet
easyJet Switzerland
El Al
Estonian Air
FedEx Express
Finnair
Germanwings
Iberia
Iberia (Air Nostrum)
Icelandair
Iceland Express
I-Fly

Jade Cargo International
Jet2
Jet4You
KLM
Kogalymavia
LOT Polish Airlines
Lufthansa
Lufthansa Cargo
Lufthansa Regional
(Eurowings)
Luxair
Malev
Medallion Air
Monarch
Niki
Nordwind Airlines
Norwegian Air Shuttle
Onur Air
Orbest Orizonia Airlines
Pakistan International
Airlines
Pegasus Airlines
Qatar Airways
Rossiya
Royal Air Maroc
Royal Air Maroc Cargo
Royal Jordanian

Ryanair	TAP Portugal	United Airlines
Scandinavian Airlines	TAP Portugal (Portugalia)	UPS Airlines
Singapore Airlines	TAROM	Ural Airlines
Sky Work Airlines	Tatarstan Airlines	US Airways
Saudi Arabian Airlines	TNT Airways	VIM Airlines
Spanair	Transaero Airlines	Vladivostok Air
Swiftair	Transavia	Vueling
Swiss European Air Lines	Tunisair	Wind Jet
Swiss International	Turkish Airlines	Wizz Air
Air Lines	Ukraine International	
TACV	Airlines	

Hotels

Best Western Hotel Alfa Aeropuerto

Calle K Entrada Mercabarna, Zona Franca, 08040 Barcelona | +34 93 33 62 564
www.bestwesternalphaaeropuerto.com

Fairly affordable and comfortable, and less than two miles from the terminal. It offers shuttles to the airport, but no views of aircraft movements from its rooms.

Tryp Barcelona Aeropuerto

Parque de Negocios Mas Blau II, Prat de Llobregat, Barcelona 08820 | +34 93 37 81 000
www.somelia.com

Slightly closer to the airport, and offering free shuttles around the clock. The hotel is smart and modern, and fairly affordable. No views of aircraft movements.

Nearby Attractions

Gerona-Costa Brava Airport

A low-cost and charter airport, dubbed Barcelona Girona by Ryanair despite being over 90km from the city. Naturally the main operator is Ryanair, however a number of business jets and charter aircraft can be seen on any given visit. Roads to either side of the terminal offer views over the runway thresholds.

Madrid Barajas Airport, Spain

MAD | LEMD
Tel: +34 91 321 1000
Web: www.aena-aeropuertos.es
Passengers: 49,863,504 (2010)

Overview

Madrid Barajas is Spain's busiest airport, and its recent expansion and increased opening to low-cost carriers saw a big rise in passengers during the latter part of the 2000s.

Madrid has always held a strong position as a hub airport for national carrier Iberia, and also as the European connection point with Latin America. It is the recent opening of bases here by both easyJet and Ryanair, and Spanish low-cost carrier Vueling that has improved access to the airport, especially to the city break and domestic market.

Enthusiasts have travelled to Madrid for the quality of movements for many years, with a number of spotting locations giving handy access. Although the influx of low-cost carriers may not interest many, they provide cheap access to spotters for quick breaks. The quality of the movements from South America often warrant a trip alone, with many of these airlines not seen elsewhere in Europe.

Naturally Iberia and its feeder airline Air Nostrum are the dominant force, along with Air Europa and Spanair. A visit of a few days will usually see the vast majority of their fleets pass through.

There are always a number of aircraft in a stored or retired state over on the storage and maintenance areas on the east side of the airfield, and keep an eye out for a preserved DC-9 outside Terminal 1 and 2.

Spotting Locations

1. Metro Station Mound

Take the Metro to Barajas, the small town adjacent to the airport. Once there, walk over the white bridge past the restaurant on the left. This raised area will allow you to log almost every movement, even aircraft using the distant new runway and Terminal 4. Excellent photography is possible of aircraft operating

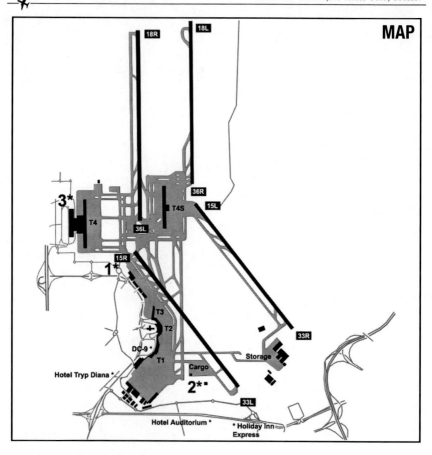

Frequencies

Tower	118.15
Tower	118.65
Tower	120.15
Tower	120.65
Ground	121.7
Ground	121.85
Ground	121.625
Ground	121.975
Ground	123.15
Clearance Delivery	130.035
Clearance Delivery	130.075
ATIS Arrival	118.25
ATIS Departure	130.85
Approach	124.025
Approach	127.5

Runways

15L/33R	11,482ft / 3,500m
15R/33L	13,451ft / 4,100m
18L/36R	11,482ft / 3,500m
18R/36L	14,268ft / 4,349m

nearer to you. It is possible to drive here if you follow signs for Barajas and then head towards the road tunnel under the airport. The mound is alongside. Various places to park exist nearby.

2. Cargo Terminals

Follow the Cargo Terminals road from the passenger terminals (do not join the motorway). This will take you past the remote ramps. Turn left at the roundabout and follow the road past the catering buildings until you reach the cargo ramp. There are places to park by the side of the road. Photography is possible here of aircraft using Runway 33L. Following the road will take you past the runway threshold, where morning shots are better, and also past the storage area.

3. Car Park P2

This car park is not the ideal spotting location, but it can yield a few of the aircraft parked on the stands around the new terminal's remote pier. Most other movements are better seen elsewhere.

Airlines

Aegean Airlines	(BA CityFlyer)	Korean Air
Aer Lingus	Brussels Airlines	LAN Airlines
Aeroflot	Bulgaria Air	LAN Ecuador
Aerolineas Argentinas	Conviasa	LAN Peru
Aeromexico	Cubana	LOT Polish Airlines
Aerosur	Czech Airlines	Lufthansa
Air Algerie	Delta Air Lines	Lufthansa Regional
Air Berlin	DHL Aviation	Luxair
Air Canada	easyJet	Malev
Air China	easyJet Switzerland	Medallion Air
Air Europa	EgyptAir	Mint Airways
Air France	El Al	Orbest Orizonia Airlines
Air Moldova	Emirates	Qatar Airways
Air Pullmantur	FedEx Feeder (Air	Royal Air Maroc
Air Transat	Contractors)	Royal Jordanian
AirBaltic	Finnair	Ryanair
Alitalia	Flyant	S7 Airlines
American Airlines	Gestair Cargo	SATA Internacional
Armavia	Hainan Airlines	Santa Barbara Airlines
Avianca	Iberia	Saudi Arabian Airlines
Blue Air	Iberia (Air Nostrum)	Scandinavian Airlines
British Airways	Icelandair	Sky Work Airlines
British Airways	KLM	Spanair

Swiss International Air Lines	Thai Airways International	Ukraine International Airlines
Syrian Air	TNT Airways	United Airlines
TACV	Transaero	UPS Airlines
TAM Airlines	Transavia	US Airways
TAP Portugal	Travel Service	Uzbekistan Airways
TAP Portugal (Portugalia)	Tunisair	Vueling
TAROM	Turkish Airlines	Wizz Air
	Turkish Airlines Cargo	

Hotels

Hotel Auditorium Madrid Airport

Avenida de Aragón 400, Madrid 28022 | +34 914 00 44 00 | www.auditoriumhoteles.com

One of the few hotels at Madrid Barajas to offer views of movements. It is situated close to runways 33L/R, and alongside the cargo apron. Rooms 2001-2114 have good views, and staff will usually help with your request for a view. Heat haze can be a problem. You can also see some arrivals into Torrejon Airport. Nearest Metro station is Canillejas, and there is a free shuttle bus.

Hotel Tryp Diana

Galeón 27, Madrid 28042 | +34 917 47 13 55 | www.solmelia.com

Situated close to the terminals, and can be very affordable. Some rooms offer views over the cargo apron, though photography is not possible. Offers a free shuttle bus to the airport.

Express by Holiday Inn Madrid Airport

Avenida de Aragón 402, Madrid 28022 | +34 917 48 16 57 | www.hiexpress.com

A little further on from the Hotel Auditorium. Has offers on rooms, which are generally affordable anyway. Some limited views of movements and cargo apron from higher rooms.

Nearby Attractions

Torrejon Airport

Torrejon is Madrid's popular executive and military airfield situated only a stone's throw away from Barajas. If you're not driving, bus line 224 heads towards Torrejon Bus Station. Further, the L4 bus from here takes you to the shopping mall (Parque Coredor) with views over the airfield. You can expect a handful of business jets and government transport aircraft on any visit. Use discretion whilst spotting here.

Cuatro-Vientos Airport

To the south west of Madrid is the small general aviation field of Cuatro-Vientos. Interestingly, this is the oldest airport in Spain, opening in 1911. Today it is popular with flight training and also has some military flights. There are always plenty of light aircraft parked here. Views of aircraft are possible from the road which leads from the terminal to the north side.

Malaga Airport, Spain

AGP | LEMG

Tel: +34 91 321 1000
Web: www.aena-aeropuertos.es
Passengers: 12,064,616 (2010)

Overview

Since the 1960s, Malaga Airport has grown to become one of the top 100 airports in the world purely on the tourist potential of the Costa del Sol, which has drawn holidaymakers from around Europe and further afield.

As with many other Spanish airports, Malaga has been continually improved upon, from the basic terminals of the 1970s which responded to the needs of charter carriers, to the newly opened structure which overshadows everything else. This new facility has turned Malaga into a true, modern gateway with ample space for growth, and it enables the airport to handle everything from low-cost airlines to high quality carriers. A new runway is set to open in early 2012, which will give Malaga more capacity.

There is a small official spotting location at the General Aviation Terminal (where there is also a museum and small collection of aircraft), but spots around the perimeter offer much better results and a nice sunny climate for your photographs. Once airside, you have some good all-round views of aircraft gates and the 14/32 runway.

Spotting Locations

1. Airport Museum

The small airport museum (see Nearby Attractions) has a viewing area on the old control tower. It is good for viewing aircraft on the executive and GA ramps, and the threshold of runway 32. Aircraft at the terminal are out of view.

2. Churriana

The small town on the southern side of the airport is the best overall area to watch aircraft at Malaga. Spotters have long come here, where a road runs part-way along the airport fence. This has now been extended to include a rough parking area. You can see most aircraft at the terminal, and all aircraft on the 14/32

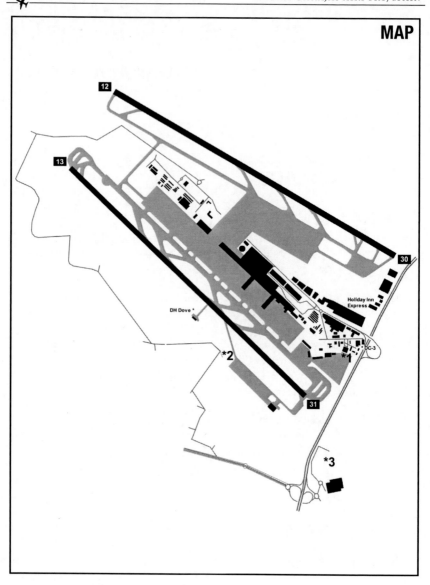

MAP

Frequencies

Ground	121.7
Clearance Delivery	121.85
ATIS	120.375
Approach	118.45
Approach	123.85
Approach	123.95

Runways

12/30 (due to open early 2012)
13/31 10,500ft / 3,200m

runway. Photography is fairly good, with the sun behind you. To reach Churriana, continue past the turn-off for the terminal and follow signs for Churriana. Soon, a road on your right leads to the fence.

3. IKEA

A short distance before touchdown on runway 32, aircraft pass over a large IKEA store. This is a good spot for photography, with a large car park and the sun behind you. To reach the store, follow directions for Churriana, but turn left towards the sea from the motorway. It is easy to spot the store.

Airlines

Aer Lingus
Aeroflot
Aigle Azur
Air Algerie
Air Arabia Maroc
Air Berlin
Air Bucharest
AirExplore
Air Europa
Air Finland
Air France (Regional)
Air Italy
Air Mediterranee
Air Transat
Airmel
Alitalia
Arkefly
Austrian Airlines
Austrian Airlines
(Lauda Air)
Avion Express
Blue Air
bmibaby
British Airways
British Airways
(BA CityFlyer)
Brussels Airlines
Bulgaria Air
Cimber Sterling
City Airline
Condor
Czech Airlines

Delta Air Lines
Eastern Airways
easyJet
easyJet Switzerland
Enter Air
Estonian Air
Europe Airpost
Finnair
Flybe
Freebird Airlines
Germanwings
Iberia
Iberia (Air Nostrum)
Icelandair
ItAli Airlines
Jet2
Jetairfly
Jettime
LOT Charters
Lufthansa
Luxair
Malev
Meridiana Fly
Mistral Air
Monarch
Neos
Niki
Norwegian Air Shuttle
Onur Air
Orbest Orizonia Airlines
Orenburg Airlines
Primera Air Scandinavia

Privilege Style
Royal Air Maroc
Royal Jordanian
Ryanair
Saudi Arabian Airlines
Scandinavian Airlines
Small Planet Airlines
SmartLynx Italia
Spanair
Strategic Airlines
Swiftair
Swiss European Air Lines
Swiss International
Air Lines
TAP Portugal (Portugalia)
Thomas Cook Airlines
Thomas Cook
Airlines Belgium
Thomson Airways
Titan Airways
Transaero Airlines
Transavia
Travel Service
(Smart Wings)
Trawel Fly
Tunisair
Turkish Airlines
VIM Airlines
Vueling
XL Airways France

Hotels

Holiday Inn Express

Avenida de Velázquez 290, 29004 Malaga | +34 952 248 500 | www.hiexpress.com

There are few hotels near Malaga Airport as most people stay in the city or resorts. This option is close to the end of both runways, but views are very limited. An SBS would help identify movements.

Nearby Attractions

Malaga Airport Museum

Aeropuerto de Málaga-junto al Terminal de Aviación General | +34 952 048 176 | www.aeroplaza.org

Hidden away near the executive and GA ramp, this museum has all manner of memorabilia from the airport and Spanish aviation, and a number of aircraft, including a DC-3 and a DC-9 nose section. Open Tuesday-Sunday 10am-2pm (and 5-8pm on Tuesday). Free entry.

Gibraltar Airport

Less than two hour's drive to the south of Malaga is the British territory of Gibraltar. A worthy tourist attraction in itself, however it's airport is one of Europe's most spectacular. With the famous Rock towering above, the short runway crosses a main road and juts into the sea. Regular flights by bmibaby, British Airways, easyJet, Monarch.

Palma de Mallorca Airport, Spain

PMI | LEPA

Tel: +34 91 321 1000
Web: www.aena-aeropuertos.es
Passengers: 21,117,270 (2010)

Overview

Palma, on the Balearic island of Mallorca, has cemented itself at the heart of one of the most popular holiday destinations in Europe. Millions flock here year-round from all over Northern Europe. Its airport is currently the third largest in Spain, and is one of the busiest in Europe during peak summer months.

All manner of charter and leisure airlines have frequented Palma since the 1960s and 70s, with the advent of the package holiday. Today this is still the case, however the low-cost airlines have muscled their way in offering cheaper flight-only deals at the cost of many charter airlines. Air Berlin in particular have become one of the largest users of the airport, having established a base at here. In addition to this, Spanish national and domestic carriers also make up a significant proportion of movements – both inter-island and to various points on the mainland.

The variety of visitors, particularly in the summer, and good weather makes Palma popular amongst spotters. Various locations around the perimeter allow for good photographs, and a number of nearby hotels have views of the movements. During the summer months weekends can prove very fruitful.

Spotting Locations

1. Runway 06R/24L Mound

Ideal for morning to mid-afternoon photography. This mound is situated alongside the runway 06R/24L. To reach it from the road to Manicor, pass the industrial estate and rental car offices, then turn down the dirt road at the first roundabout.

2. Perimeter Road

The road running alongside runway 06L/24R is good for afternoon photography and logging. This is also off the road from Palma to Manicor, turning right before the first service station and down the track on the left as the road enters a hairpin. There are plenty of parking spots and benches along the track.

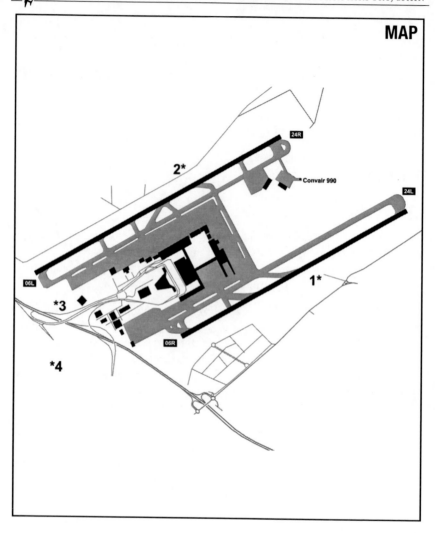

MAP

24R

2*

Convair 990

24L

06L

*3

1*

*4

06R

Frequencies

Tower 118.45
Operations 130.25
Ground North 121.9
Ground South 121.7
Clearance Delivery ..121.6
ATIS......................119.25
Approach 118.95
Approach 119.15
Approach 119.4

Runways

06L/24R   10,728ft / 3,270m
06R/24L   9,842ft / 3,000m

3. Perimeter

If photography is not an immediate concern, it is possible to walk around the airport complex and perimeter to log all aircraft parked on the various ramps. The car rental car parks are a good place to start. The area is large, however, so it's best to explore by car.

4. Beach

When arrivals are coming from the sea, as they often do, the nearby beach is fine for logging and some photography of arrivals.

Airlines

Adria Airways	Iberia
Aer Lingus	Iberia (Air Nostrum)
Air Algerie	Jat Airways
Air Berlin	Jet2
Air Europa	Jetairfly
Air Mediterranee	Lufthansa
Air One	Luxair
AlbaStar	Malev
Aviogenex	Meridiana Fly
Arkefly	Monarch
bmi British Midland	Neos
bmibaby	Niki
British Airways (BA CityFlyer)	Norwegian Air Shuttle
Brussels Airlines	Onur Air
Bulgaria Air	Orbest Orizonia Airlines
City Airline	Ryanair
Cimber Sterling	S7 Airlines
Condor	Scandinavian Airlines
Darwin Airline	Sky Work Airlines
easyJet	Small Planet Airlines
easyJet Switzerland	Spanair
Edelweiss Air	Swiss European Air Lines
Enter Air	Swiss International Air Lines
Europe Airpost	TAROM
Finnair	Thomas Cook Airlines
Flybe	Thomas Cook Airlines Belgium
Germanwings	Thomas Cook Airlines Scandinavia
Helvetic Airways	Thomson Airways
Holidays Czech Airlines	Transavia

Transavia France
Travel Service
Travel Service (Smart Wings)
TUIfly
TUIfly Nordic

VIM Airlines
Vueling
Wizz Air
XL Airways Germany

Hotels

Hotel Marina Luz

07610 Cala Estancia, Mallorca | +34 952 05 88 82 | www.hotel-marina-luz.com

Probably the most popular hotel at Palma with spotters, located in Ca'n Pastilla. Its rooms have great views of aircraft on approach to the runways, and is a short walk from spotting locations. Ask for a top-floor room facing the Bay of Palma for the best views. This is an adult-only hotel.

Hotel Helios

Carre Pollacra 5, 07610 Palma (Mallorca) | +34 971 26 44 00 | www.helios-hotels.com

Airport facing rooms on the 5th floor have excellent views from balconies of the traffic on runways 06L/R, and many of the ground movements and aprons. The hotel is very affordable, even in summer.

Nearby Attractions

Son Bonnet Airport

The other airfield on Mallorca is Son Bonnet, situated a few miles northwest of Palma city. It is a general aviation airfield with a number of resident aircraft and the occasional larger movement. A preserved DC-3 can be found here as a gate guardian, registered N330. Views can be had from various places around the fence, and through hangar windows.

Tenerife South Airport, Spain (Canary Islands)

TFS | GCTS

Tel: +34 91 321 10 00
Web: www.aena-aeropuertos.es
Passengers: 7,300,000 (2010)

Overview

Tenerife South is the newer of two airports on the island. It is the busier of the two and used by many of the charter and low-cost airlines from Europe, and a fair number of scheduled flights from the mainland. In the summer months it can be quite busy, with airlines from different countries generally arriving on different days. The winter months are still fairly busy given the year-round warm climate.

Most visitors to the island stay in the nearby resorts, but there are a number of spots around the airport to take advantage of the sunshine and photograph airliners.

Spotting Locations

1. Runway 26 South Side

If you travel past the airport turn-off on the motorway, take the next junction towards the sea, turning right and then right again at the petrol station. Eventually this small road leads past the end of runway 26, and you can find a spot where the view suits you. If 26 is in use, you can get shots of aircraft landing and lining up.

2. Runway 08

From the terminal head west on the motorway and take the first exit on TF65, then take the road to Abrigal. When you see the concrete pillars, turn right and you'll reach the runway threshold. This is a good spot for photography of aircraft both landing and lining up when using 08.

3. Children's Play Area

Near the domestic terminal is a children's play area with some views of the executive ramp and taxiway beyond. It is not great for photography, but can help you log some of the airport's visitors.

MAP

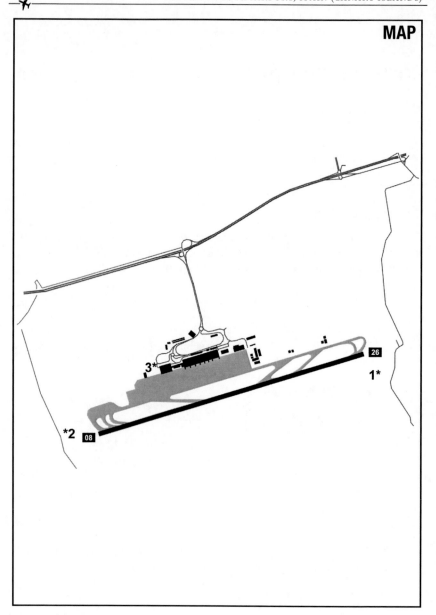

Frequencies

Ground...................121.9
ATIS...................118.675
Approach...............120.3
Approach...............127.7

Runway

08/26   10,498ft / 3,200m

Airlines

Aer Lingus	KMV Avia
Air Berlin	Luxair
Air Europa	Meridiana Fly
Air Finland	Monarch
airBaltic	Neos
Austrian Airlines (Lauda Air)	Niki
Binter Canarias (Naysa)	Norwegian Air Shuttle
Bulgaria Air	Orbest Orizonia Airlines
Cimber Air Sterling	Ryanair
Condor	Small Planet Airlines
easyJet	Spanair
easyJet Switzerland	TAROM
Edelweiss Air	Thomson Airways
Europe Airpost	Thomas Cook Airlines
Germania	Thomas Cook Airlines Scandinavia
Germanwings	Transaero Airlines
Finnair	Transavia
Iberia	Transavia France
I-Fly	Travel Service
Islas Airways	TUIfly
Jet2	VIM Airlines
Jetairfly	

Hotels

Hotel Aguamarina Golf

Avda. del Atlántico, 2, Urbanización Golf del Sur, San Miguel de Abona, 38620, Tenerife
+34 922 738999 | http://www.hotelaguamarinagolf.com

Probably the best hotel for views of movements at Tenerife South, with views of aircraft approaching and departing. The hotel is around two miles from the airport, next to the sea.

Cordial Golf Plaza Hotel

Urb.Golf del sur 38620, San Miguel de Abona, Tenerife | +34 922 73 70 00
www.cordialcanarias.com/en/cordial_golf_plaza.html

This hotel is a nice place to stay and has views of aircraft approaching runway 08. The Plane Spotting Hotels website states rooms 131-138 and 230-236 are good for noting aircraft registrations. You can also take good photos from the pool area and some balconies.

Nearby Attractions

Tenerife North Los Rodeos Airport

The older Tenerife Airport, situated close to Santa Cruz in the north of the island. It is much quieter, but enjoys more scheduled traffic from the mainland, including some large widebody aircraft. It also sees some charter and cargo traffic. You can spot from some areas around the terminal, and watch out for a stored Vickers Viscount.

Santa Cruz de Tenerife Museum

Calle de San Isidro, Santa Cruz de Tenerife | +34 922 22 16 58

A small military museum with a couple of preserved helicopters. Open 10am-2pm, Tuesday-Saturday.

Airports in Sweden

1. Stockholm Arlanda

This page has been intentionally left blank.

Stockholm Arlanda Airport, Sweden

ARN | ESSA

Tel: +46 87 976 000
Web: www.arlanda.se
Passengers: 16,962,416 (2010)

Overview

Stockholm's main airport at Arlanda opened in 1960 and is some 26 miles north of the city. It was built to replace the crowded Bromma airport as the city's main gateway. The airport is one of the hubs of Scandinavian Airline System (SAS).

Arlanda has four terminals. Terminals 3 and 4 are used for domestic flights, whilst 2 and 5 are used for international flights. All terminals are joined together, and the central Sky City area was built as a communal area with places to eat, shop and relax, with large windows looking out over the runways. There are also a number of cargo facilities and hangars at the airport.

There are three runways at Arlanda – the most recent opening in 2003. Enthusiasts are catered for near the recently-built runway 01L/19R with a covered building known as the Shed. Elsewhere views are possible around the airport.

The vast majority of movements at Arlanda are operated by Norwegian Air Shuttle and SAS, including some by the long-haul fleet. Most European carriers frequent the airport, and a number of long haul airlines provide links with North America, Asia and the Middle East. Cargo carriers are also prominent, and if you explore a little you can find no fewer than four Caravelle aircraft stored at the airport.

Spotting Locations

1. Spotters Shed

A popular official location provided for the viewing of aircraft is a hut at the northern end of Runway 01R/19L. It also has views over parts of runway 08/26, and the de-icing area. You can't see any of the terminal stands. Aircraft can be seen at close quarters when landing on runway 19L and taxying past. You can drive to the spot, or take bus line 593 from Terminal 5.

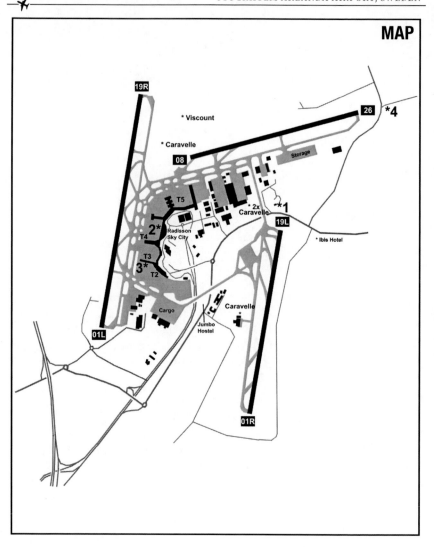

MAP

Frequencies

Tower	123.1
Tower	125.125
Ground	121.7
Ground	121.925
Ground	121.975
Clearance Delivery	121.825
ATIS Arrival	119.0
ATIS Departure	121.625
Control	123.75

Runways

01L/19R 10,830ft / 3,301m
01R/19L 8,201ft / 2,500m
08/26 8,202ft / 2,500m

2. Sky City

The Sky City is located between terminals 4 and 5. It has large windows around the food court area which look out on to the aprons and Runway 01L/19R. The glass can make photography difficult, but logging aircraft is not a problem. A mezzanine area has comfy seats to enjoy the view from.

3. Terminal 3

Terminal 3 is simply a pier with a couple of gates from which most domestic commuter aircraft depart. Before going through security, there are windows on either side of the pier from which you can see most movements around terminals 2, 3 and 4. You can also see across to the cargo ramp and business ramp.

4. Runway 26

Driving away from the airport, instead of taking the motorway to Stockholm, turn left on the 273 and head past the Spotters Shed. Just before the Ibis Hotel, turn left past the lake and follow the road until you can see the runway approach lights. Turn right onto a gravel road and park up. This is a perfect spot for photographs if aircraft are using runway 26.

Airlines

Adria Airways	(BA CityFlyer)	Hoga Kusten Fly
Aeroflot	British Airways	(Golden Air)
Aerosvit Airlines	World Cargo	Iberia
Air Aland	Cathay Pacific Cargo	Icelandair
AirBaltic	China Airlines Cargo	Iceland Express
Air Berlin	Cimber Sterling	Iran Air
Air Caraibes	Corendon Airlines	Iraqi Airways
Air China	Czech Airlines	Jat Airways
Al-Naser Airlines	Delta Air Lines	Jetpak
(Jordan Aviation)	DHL	KLM
Amapola Flyg	easyJet Switzerland	Korean Air Cargo
Arkia Israel Airlines	Estonian Air	LOT Polish Airlines
Austrian Airlines	Estonian Air Regional	Lufthansa
Austrian Arrows	Ethiopian Airlines	Lufthansa Regional
B&H Airlines	Europe Airpost	Malev
BH Air	FedEx Express	NextJet
Belavia	Finnair	Niki
Blue1	Fly Hellas	Norwegian Air Shuttle
Blue1 (Golden Air)	Germanwings	Qatar Airways
British Airways	Golden Air	Pegasus Airlines
British Airways	Gotlandsflyg (NextJet)	Primera Air

Rossiya	Spanair	Turkish Airlines
Royal Falcon	SunExpress	Turkish Airlines
SATA International	Swiss International	(Anadolujet)
Scandinavian Airlines	Air Lines	United Airlines
Skyways Express	Syrian Air	UPS Airlines
Skyways Expres	TAP Portugal	West Air
(Direktflyg)	Thai Airways International	

Hotels

Radisson SAS Sky City Hotel

Stockholm Arlanda Airport, SE-190 45 | +46 8 50 67 40 00 | www.radissonsas.com

Located above the terminals and linked into the Sky City area. Rooms higher up and at each end of the building offer great views over the movements – particularly of Runway 01L/19R. Photography is not really possible, however. The hotel can be expensive.

Hotel Ibis Stockholm Arlanda

Lindskrog, vag 273, S-190 45 Arlanda | +46 86 55 01 00 | www.ibishotel.com

Offers shuttle to the terminal, which takes 10 minutes. The hotel is fairly affordable. Some rooms have distant views of aircraft using runway 19L. SBS users will have more luck identifying aircraft.

Jumbo Stay Hostel

Jumbovägen 4, 190 47 Stockholm Arlanda | +46 8 593 604 00 | www.jumbostay.se

A unique high-end hostel inside a former Pan Am Boeing 747-200 (last registration 3D-NEE). It is situated just off the airport link road, close to the cargo terminal and a taxiway. Rooms are comfortable and most have views of some movements, but photography is not possible. Wi-fi internet is free of charge.

Nearby Attractions

Bromma Airport

This was the original airport for Stockholm, but limitations in its facilities saw most scheduled traffic move to Arlanda by 1983. Today it is used extensively by regional services by the likes of Malmö Aviation, Next Jet, Golden Air and Skyways, plus many business jets. There is a viewing area on high ground above the terminal, and an aviation shop selling books and models inside. Roads around the perimeter are also good for watching movements. A Convair 580 can be found on the south side of the runway, and a preserved (airworthy) DC-3 in SAS colours is also based here.

Stockholm-Skavsta Airport

A low-cost airport 65 miles south of Stockholm at Nyköping. It handles flights by Ryanair, TUIfly Nordic and Wizz Air amongst others. There are some places to view movements around the terminal and at either end of the main runway.

Airports in Switzerland

1. Geneva
2. Zurich

This page has been intentionally left blank.

Geneva Airport, Switzerland

GVA | LSGG

Tel: +41 22 717 71 11
Web: www.gva.ch
Passengers: 11,785,522 (2010)

Overview

Geneva's airport is located in the area of Cointrin to the north of the city. A landing strip has existed here since the 1920s, though major expansion was undertaken after World War II, and again in the 1960s to cope with a massive growth in air travel to the city.

The fairly unique system of remote satellites with their own aircraft gates, linked by underground passage to the main terminal, is still in use today allowing good management of the limited space available. Without this, congestion in busy periods would become unmanageable.

Since 1956, an exchange of territory has been agreed with France, whereby the terminal allows passengers destined for France to exit via different channels and ultimately onto the road heading straight to the nearby French border. For departing passengers, a separate area of the terminal has been set aside for those travelling to France. Naturally Air France is the dominant user of this area.

Geneva is very much an international city, with organisations based here including the European headquarters of the United Nations. There are also many conferences held in Geneva annually. This all bodes very well for the airport, which as a result handles more business jet movements than most other European airports, and is also high on the list of most European airlines. Additionally during the colder winter months, Geneva plays host to an influx of leisure passengers destined for the nearby ski resorts in the Alps. Sadly for the enthusiast, the excellent viewing gallery remains closed.

Spotting Locations

1. Runway 23

When aircraft are arriving over the lake, follow the road from the terminal towards Cargo-Fret. After a u-turn to join the highway, go under the Palexpo convention centre in the direction of Ferney. After passing over the highway again,

MAP

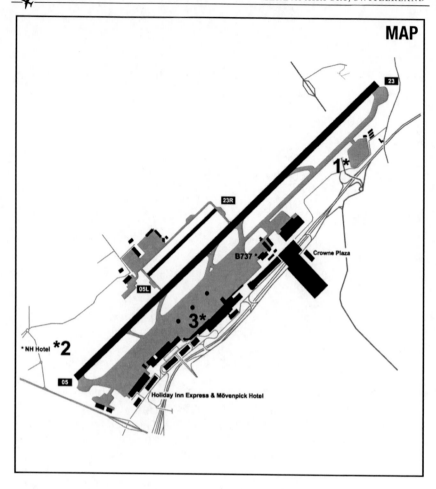

Frequencies

Tower	119.7
Tower	119.9
Apron	121.75
Apron	121.85
Ground	121.675
Departure	119.525
Arrival	136.25
ATIS	124.75
ATIS	135.575
Approach Final	120.3
Approach	121.3
Approach	131.325
Approach	136.45

Runways

05/23 12,795ft / 3,900m
05L/23R 2,700 / 823m (Grass)

turn left at the lights and then stay to the right. You will see the barracks and an embankment, which offers elevated views over the runway and taxiway. Bus route 28 from the terminal passes this spot in the direction of Jardin Botanique. Get off at Tunnel Routier stop. You can also see aircraft parked on the eastern storage ramp from this area.

2. Runway 05

At the Runway 05 end, leave the terminal and head for Meyrin, past the World Trade Center. Turn right at the lights for Meyrin, and then turn right at the Tag Aviation signpost. After a u-turn, you will pass some buildings before the road turns left. Park in the car park on the right and then walk back in the direction you came from, and down a pedestrian path which leads to a fence near the runway threshold. Bus 28 to Hopital La Tour leaves the terminal in this direction. Alight at Blandonnet and walk towards Tag Aviation and the pedestrian path.

3. Inside Terminal

There are still some views inside the terminal from the top floor (where the old viewing deck used to be). Find the Altitude cafe and you'll notice the windows. The floor below also has some views.

Airlines

Aer Lingus
Aeroflot
AirBridgeCargo Airlines
Air Algerie
Air Canada
Air Europa
Air France
Air France (Regional)
Air Malta
Air Mauritius
Alitalia
Austrian Arrows
Baboo
Belair
Blue Islands
bmibaby
British Airways
British Airways
(BA Cityflyer)
Brussels Airlines

Czech Connect Airlines
Darwin Airline
DHL Aviation
easyJet
easyJet Switzerland
EgyptAir
El Al
Edelweiss Air
Emirates
Etihad Airways
Finnair
Finnair (Flybe Nordic)
Gulf Air
Iberia
Iceland Express
Iran Air
Jade Cargo International
Jet2
Jet4you
KLM

KLM CityHopper
Kuwait Airways
LOT Polish Airlines
Lufthansa
Lufthansa Regional
Lufthansa Regional
(Augsburg Airways)
Lufthansa Regional
(Eurowings)
Luxair
Middle East Airlines
Monarch
Nouvelair
Norwegian Air Shuttle
Qatar Airways
Royal Air Maroc
Saudi Arabian Airlines
Scandinavian Airlines
Skyways
Swiss European Air Lines

Swiss International
Air Lines
TAP Portugal
Thomas Cook Airlines
Thomson Airways
TNT Airways

Transavia
Tunisair
Turkish Airlines
Twin Jet
Ukraine International
Airlines

United Airlines
UPS Airlines (Farnair
Switzerland)
Uzbekistan Airways

Hotels

Crowne Plaza Geneva Airport

34 Route Francoise-Peyrot, Geneva 1218 | +41 22 74 70 202 | www.crowneplaza.com

Situated within walking distance of the terminal building. Has very few views of aircraft movements, and can be expensive at certain times of year.

Express by Holiday Inn

Route de Pre-Bois 16, Geneva 1215 | +41 22 93 93 939 | www.holidayinn.com

Situated alongside the major motorway, and also next to one of the business jet ramps. Some of the higher rooms have views of the action. Free shuttle to the terminal.

Mövenpick Hotel Geneva Airport

Route de Pre-Bois 20, Geneva 1215 | +41 22 71 71 111 | www.moevenpick-hotels.com

Situated alongside the Holiday Inn, and sometimes more affordable. Again, some higher rooms offer views of aircraft, although these can be limited. Free shuttle to the terminal.

NH Geneva Airport Hotel

Av. De Mategnin 21, Geneva 1217 | +41 22 98 99 000 | www.nh-hotels.com

One of the best-placed hotels at Geneva Airport for the enthusiast. Although not all rooms offer views, the ones that do face the threshold of Runway 05. The hotel is also close to the spotting location at this end of the runway.

Nearby Attractions

Annecy Airport

A small regional airport with Air France links to Paris Orly, and a busy GA scene. Situated around 25 miles from Geneva in France. You can see most aircraft from around the terminal area, or the road which passes the end of the runway.

Zurich Kloten Airport, Switzerland

ZRH | LSZH

Tel: +41 43 816 22 11
Web: www.zurich-airport.com
Passengers: 22,900,00 (2010)

Overview

Zurich is a popular choice in Europe for aviation enthusiasts as it provides some excellent facilities, and has been the home of a well-stocked enthusiasts' shop for many years.

The airport is the busiest in Switzerland, yet it serves neither the capital city nor a particularly large local population. It is the main operating base for national carrier Swiss International Air Lines, and its various subsidiaries. Other airlines from across Europe, North America and Asia make up the numbers with daily flights, and an interesting mix of executive jets regularly occupy the ramps.

Every January, the World Economic Forum is held close to Zurich in the town of Davos. This brings in leaders from around the world, and their entourages of private jets, both big and small. Enthusiasts flock to the airport every year for the feast of rare types and registrations.

The official viewing locations at Zurich are amongst the best in Europe. There are, however, some useful spots around the airport which can produce stunning photographs. Whilst movements are not as numerous as other European hubs, Zurich is worth a visit to clear the Swiss fleet in a short time.

Spotting Locations

1. Pier B Terrace

The terrace on top of Pier B is the original and best spot for watching and logging aircraft movements at Zurich. Aircraft pass by and park very close to this location, making photography possible. The BUCHairSHOP is located here, along with a restaurant and refreshments. This terrace is signposted within the terminal.

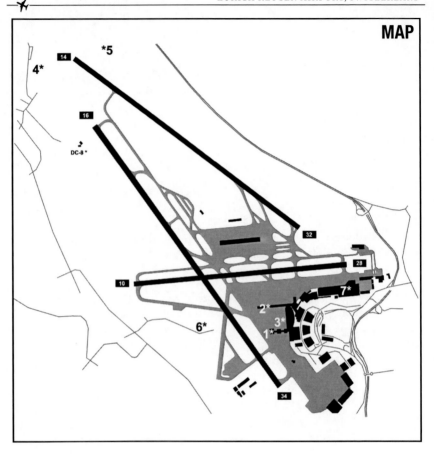

Frequencies

Tower	119.7
Tower	120.225
Terminal	127.75
Apron South	121.75
Apron North	121.85
Ground	118.1
Ground	119.7
Ground	121.9
Departure	125.95
Clearance Delivery	121.8
ATIS	128.525
Approach	118.0
Approach	119.7
Approach	120.75
Approach	125.325

Runways

10/28	8,202ft / 2,500m
14/32	10,827ft / 3,300m
16/34	12,139ft / 3,700m

2. Pier E Terrace

Another rooftop terrace, Pier E brings you a little closer to the runways and some of the gates not visible from Pier B. Photography is good. This position is reached via bus from the Pier B Terrace. There is an additional CHF4 charge for adults, CHF2 for children. This terrace is not open every day.

3. Guided Tours

A behind-the-scenes bus tour is available at Zurich. This leaves from the Pier B Terrace and takes in the Airside Centre, Piers A and B, Runway 28, nature reserve, cargo and maintenance areas, and the emergence services. Tour lasts over an hour and costs CHF8 for adults and CHF4 for children. Tickets can be bought from the terrace or through the website www.zurich-airport.com

4. Runways 14 and 16

Two runways end close to each other at the far end of the airport to the terminal. Drive in the direction of Oberglatt. A short distance after this small town, find the large car park on your right. This spot can produce some stunning photographs with the mountains as a backdrop. It is best in the afternoon, and this spot is popular with locals.

5. Runway 14

Continue past the previous spot and turn right along a small road which leads to another car park. This spot allows better photography of aircraft on approach in the mornings.

6. Perimeter Fence

Opposite the terminal and Runway 16/34 is another famed spot at Zurich. It pits you amongst the action, with great views of traffic on the runways, and aircraft around the terminals. Photography is excellent from the afternoon, even with shorter lenses. To reach the spot, drive towards Oberglatt, but turn right just before the pedestrian bridge at Rümlang Station. Alternatively, bus route 510 from Car Park F leaves every hour. Get off at Rumlang Station. From Rümlang, walk through the tunnel, cross the footbridge and keep walking until you see the fence.

7. Car Park F

The top level of Car Park F gives good views over the commuter ramp and Runway 28 threshold and taxiways. Photography is good in the late morning and early afternoon from this spot.

Airlines

Adria Airways
Aer Lingus
Aeroflot
airBaltic
Air Berlin
Air Canada
Air Malta
Air France (CityJet)
American Airlines
Austrian Airlines
Austrian Arrows
Belair
Belle Air
B&H Airlines
Blue1
Blue Islands
bmi Regional
British Airways
British Airways (BA CityFlyer)
Bulgaria Air
Cirrus Airlines
City Airline
Croatia Airlines
Cyprus Airways
Czech Airlines
Delta Air Lines
easyJet
Edelweiss Air
El Al
Emirates
Finnair
Freebird Airlines
Germanwings
Hainan Airlines
Hello
Helvetic Airways
Iberia
InterSky
Jat Airways

KLM
Korean Air
LOT Polish Airlines
Lufthansa
Lufthansa Regional
Lufthansa Regional (Augsburg Airways)
Lufthansa Regional (Eurowings)
Malev
Montenegro Airlines
Niki
OLT
Oman Air
Pegasus Airlines
Pegasus Airlines (IZair)
Qatar Airways
Royal Air Maroc
Royal Jordanian
Scandinavian Airlines
Singapore Airlines
Sky Airlines
SriLankan Airlines
Sun Express
Swiss European Air Lines
Swiss International Air Lines
Swiss (Contact Air)
Swiss (Darwin Airline)
Swiss (Helvetic Airways)
Swiss (PrivatAir)
TAP Portugal
Thai Airways International
Tunisair
Turkish Airlines
Ukraine International Airlines
United Airlines
US Airways
Vueling

Hotels

Park Inn Zurich Airport

Flughofstrasse 75, 8153 Rümlang | +41 44 828 8686 | www.zurich-airport.parkinn.com

If you request a room overlooking the airport, you won't be disappointed. Most of the action is visible from here, although photography is a little limited due to the distance and glass. This hotel can be fairly expensive.

NH Zurich Airport Hotel

Schaffhauserstrasse 101, 8152 Glattbrugg, Zurich | +41 44 808 5000 | www.nh-hotels.com

Very affordable hotel a short distance from the terminals. Some rooms offer limited views of movements on Runway 16, but no photographic opportunities.

Nearby Attractions

Dübendorf Airfield Museum of Military Aviation

Überlandstrasse 255, 8600 Dübendorf | +41 44 823 2017 | www.ju-air.ch

A popular museum only a few miles from Zurich Airport. Has a number of military aircraft preserved in hangars. Also the opportunity to experience sightseeing flights on a restored Junkers Ju-52 aircraft.

This page has been intentionally left blank.

Airports in Turkey

1. Istanbul Ataturk

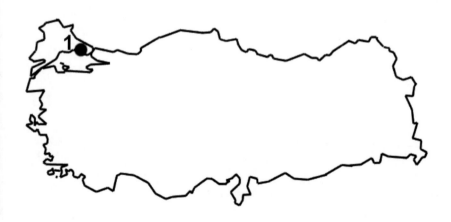

This page has been intentionally left blank.

Istanbul Ataturk Airport, Turkey

IST | LTBA

Tel: +90 212 463 3000
Web: www.ataturkairport.com
Passengers: 32,145,619 (2010)

Overview

Ataturk is Istanbul's main airport, situated on the European side of the city. It has three runways in an L-shaped pattern, and two passenger terminals. There is also a fairly busy cargo terminal.

Traffic comprises a good mix of European and long-haul flights, with the vast majority made up of the based Turkish Airlines and AtlasJet. Things are set to get busier if plans by the national airline come to fruition, with 60 more Boeing 737-800's on order at the time of writing. The aim is to replicate the hubs at Dubai and Doha in linking East/West passengers in waves.

There are a number of opportunities to spot around the perimeter, and a nice aviation museum on the southern boundary. It is also worth visiting the busy Sabiha Gökçen Airport on the Asian side of the city.

Spotting Locations

1. Flynn Shopping Mall

Located across the road from the two 17/35 runways, close to the 36 end. This shopping mall has a balcony which you can use as it is part of a café area. This is a wonderful place to spot from, and perfect for taking pictures of aircraft on the near runways. You can also see arrivals and departures on the other runway, and aircraft parked at the terminal and cargo ramps.

2. Runway 17 Arrivals

If aircraft are arriving on runways 17L/R, there is a bridge over the motorway which you can use. It is a good spot for photographing aircraft, and also offers some views of the storage ramp nearby.

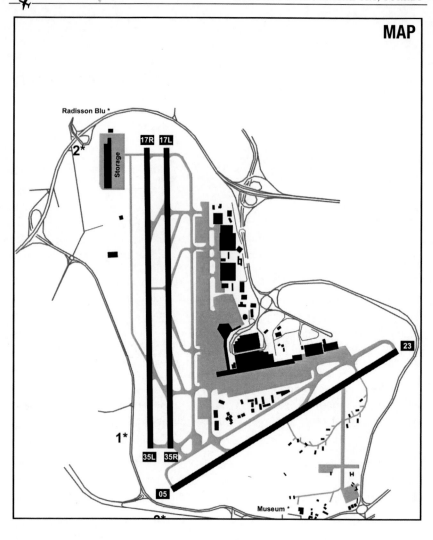

MAP

Frequencies

Tower	121.8
Tower	122.325
Ground	121.8
Ground	121.9
Clearance Delivery	121.7
ATIS	128.2
Approach	120.5
Approach	121.1

Runways

05/23	7,546ft	2,600m
17L/35R	9,843ft	3,000m
17R/35L	9,843ft	3,000m

3. IBB Florya Park

This public park is located alongside the sea close to the end of runway 05. It is good for watching arrivals on 05 and 35L/R, and can be good for photographs when the sun is in the right position. The nearby Kelesoglu Business Centre also has a balcony on the third floor which can be used without question.

Airlines

ACT Airlines	Donbassaero	Pegasus Airlines (IZair)
Adria Airways	Dniproavia	Polet Airlines
Aegean Airlines	EgyptAir	Qatar Airways
Aeroflot	Emirates	Red Wings Airlines
Aerosvit Airlines	Etihad Airways	Rossiya
Air Algerie	Eurex Cargo	Royal Air Maroc
Air Astana	FedEx Express	Royal Jordanian
Air France	(MNG Airlines)	Saudi Arabian Airlines
Air France Cargo	Gulf Air	SCAT
(MNG Airlines)	Hainan Airlines	Silk Way Airlines
Air Malta	Hamburg Airways	Singapore Airlines
Air Moldova	Iberia	Sky Airlines
Air Transat	Iraqi Airways	SkyExpress
airBaltic	Jade Cargo International	Somon Air
Albanian Airlines	Jat Airways	Swiss International
Alitalia	Jupiter Airlines	Air Lines
Armavia	Jetairfly	Syrian Air
Asiana Airlines	Kish Air	TAROM
AtlasJet	KLM	Tatarstan Airlines
Austrian Airlines	Korean Air	TNT Airways
Austrian Arrows	Kuban Airlines	Tunis Air
Azerbaijan Airlines	Kuwait Airways	Turkish Airlines
Azmar Airlines	Kyrgyzstan Airlines	Turkish Airlines Cargo
Belavia	Libyan Airlines	Turkmenistan Airlines
B&H Airlines	LOT Polish Airlines	ULS Airlines Cargo
British Airways	Lufthansa	UPS Airlines
Buraq Air	Medallion Air	(MNG Airlines)
Carpatair	Mahan Air	Uzbekistan Airlines
Caspian Airlines	Malaysia Airlines	Uzbekistan Airlines Cargo
China Southern Airlines	Malev	Viking Hellas
Corendon Airlines	Middle East Airlines	Wind Rose Aviation
Croatia Airlines	MNG Airlines	
Delta Air Lines	Nouvelair	
DHL (MNG Airlines)	Olympic Air	
Donavia	Onur Air	

Hotels

Radisson Blu Airport Hotel

E-5 Karayolu (yanyol) No: 20 - Sefakoy Kavsagi - K. Cekmece - 34295 Istanbul | +90 (212) 411 38 38
www.radissonblu.com/hotel-istanbulairport

A perfect place to stay if you can get a room overlooking the airport. You'll be able to see all movements on the 18L/36R runway, and many around the terminal area, plus the GA area. Rooms are not good for photographs, however.

Nearby Attractions

Hava Kuvvetleri Museum

Komutanligi 34149 Yesilköy – ISTANBUL | +90 212 663 24 90 | www.hho.edu.tr/muze/muze.htm

A nice aircraft museum on the south side of the airport. It has a number of warplanes and airliners in its collection, including a Viscount and Caravelle. The museum is open Wednesday-Sunday from 9am-4.30pm. There is an entrance fee, and a separate fee if you want to take photographs. The museum has a car park, and is also near the Yesilköy train station, which is served from the city centre.

Istanbul Sabiha Gökçen Airport

The city's other main airport, situated across the Bosphorus in Asian Turkey. This has grown significantly in recent years, and is home to airlines such as Pegasus and MNG Cargo. It currently handles around 11.5 million passengers per year, mainly consisting of cargo and low-cost flights.

Airports in Ukraine

1. Kiev Borispol

This page has been intentionally left blank.

Kiev Borispol Airport, Ukraine

KBP | UKBB

Tel: +380 44 363 77 77
Web: www.kbp.aero
Passengers: 6,700,000 (2010)

Overview

Borispol is the largest and busiest airport in Ukraine, and one of three serving the capital Kiev. It has grown into a busy hub for the region, and is served by carriers from across Europe, Russia and the CIS. It has usually has a tempting array of aircraft belonging to the government scattered around the field, but these can be difficult to see unless you are travelling in or out by aircraft.

The airport's main terminals are B and F. The original Terminal A is currently closed, and Terminal C is for VIP passengers only. Terminal D is under construction, scheduled to be opened imminently. Terminal E is also planned for opening in 2015. A third runway is set to be constructed between 2012-2014.

No official viewing areas exist at Borispol, but spotting is possible if you are discrete, both from around the airport and within the terminal once airside. Whether it is possible to see movements from the new terminal remains to be seen.

Spotting Locations

1. New Terminal Area

To the north of the new terminal site is a field which has not yet been developed, but may be in the future. At the moment you can reach this area by walking north on the main road, then across the field towards the fence. You can see and photograph aircraft using runway 18L/36R, and also see movements on the other runway.

2. Eastern Boundary

Track on the eastern boundary of the airport lead you up to the airport fence, from where you can get views of aircraft using runway 18L/36R, and the terminal areas. It is best if you have the use of a car as it is too far to walk to this location.

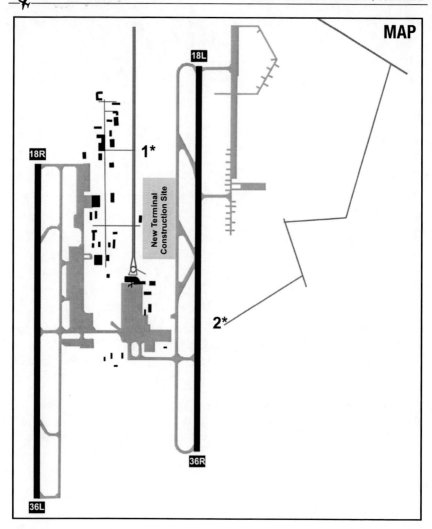

Frequencies

Tower	119.65
Tower	124.0
Radar	120.9
Radar	124.675
Radar	127.725
Radar	128.175
Ops	131.775
Ground	118.05
Delivery	130.275
ATIS	126.7

Runways

18L/36R	13,123ft / 4,000m
18R/36L	11,483ft / 3,500m

Airlines

Adria Airways
Aero Charter
Aeroflot
Aerosvit Airlines
Air Arabia
Air France
Air Moldova
airBaltic
Alitalia
Arkia Israel Airlines
Armavia
Astra Airlines
Austrian Airlines
Austrian Arrows
Azerbaijan Airlines
Belavia
British Airways
Caspian Airlines
Czech Airlines
DHL Express
Dniproavia
Donavia
Donbassaero
El Al
Estonian Air
Finnair

Flydubai
Georgian Airways
Kalitta Air
KLM
Libyan Airlines
LOT Polish Airlines
Lufthansa
Lufthansa Regional
Motor Sich Airlines
Malev
Orenair
Rossiya
Royal Jordanian
RusLine
S7 Airlines
Transaero Airlines
Turkish Airlines
Turkmenistan Airlines
Ukraine International Airlines
Ural Airlines
UM Airlines
UTair Aviation
Uzbekistan Airways
Volga-Dnepr
Wind Jet
Wind Rose Aviation

Hotels

There are no hotels in the immediate vicinity of Borispol Airport.

Nearby Attractions

Zhulyany Airport

This is the original airport of Kiev, and located much closer to the city centre. It is fairly compact, and home to the Ukraine State Aviation Museum (see below). Although Zhulyany operated as a domestic airport for many years, today it handles international flights too, since Wizz Air relocated there. Like Borispol, it is hard to spot from unless you are travelling through the airport. You can see some aircraft on the move if you visit the museum.

Ukraine State Aviation Museum

1 Medova street, Kiev, 03048 | +38 044 4518314 | www.zhulyany.net

This is the largest aviation museum in Ukraine, and well worth a visit if you are in the city. It is located next to Zhulyany Airport, and has a vast array of mainly Soviet aircraft - around 70 in total. These range from fighter jets to large helicopters and airliners, including the TU-104, IL-18 and IL-62. The museum is open daily from 10am-7pm (10am-4.30pm October-March).

Gostomel Airport

Kiev's cargo airport, situated 15 miles north west of the city centre. It is the place to see large AN-12 and AN-225 aircraft. It is useful to have a car to explore the roads around the airport in order to see movements.

Airports in United Kingdom and Republic of Ireland

1. Dublin
2. East Midlands
3. London City
4. London Gatwick
5. London Heathrow
6. London Luton
7. London Stansted
8. Manchester

This page has been intentionally left blank.

Dublin Airport, Republic of Ireland

DUB | EIDW
Tel: +353 1 814 1111
Web: www.dublinairport.com
Passengers: 18,431,265 (2010)

Overview

When built in 1940, the terminal at Dublin's airport was considered to be the best in Europe and won architectural accolades for its designer. Following the Second World War, the number of services increased rapidly. Three hard runways were laid, and new hangars and other buildings built. A terminal extension could only cope a few years into the long-haul jet revolution, and in 1972 another new building was opened with a capacity of 1.6 million passengers per year. The current main runway 10/28 was opened in 1989.

With the general rise in passenger numbers due to popular routes to London and New York came also the low-cost boom. Local carrier Ryanair dramatically boosted passenger figures with its cheap flights to the UK and Europe, and today has a massive base here, although it has somewhat reduced operations in defiance of the imposed passenger tax. The passenger terminal has required steady expansion, and in 2006 opened its new pier to alleviate pressure.

Sadly no official spotting facilities remain at Dublin, but a number of locations around the perimeter are popular.

Spotting Locations

1. Southern Perimeter

Following the road away from the terminal, turn on to Old Airport Road, which follows the perimeter. You'll soon be alongside the main runway, and depending on the direction in use you can find a raised spot which will put you alongside the touchdown zone. Many spotters congregate here. Photography is good, and all traffic will pass you eventually. Follow the road around for spots on the northern side of the runway. Buses heading for Dublin will drop you ½ a mile from this location (Dardistown Cemetery). A car is recommended.

MAP

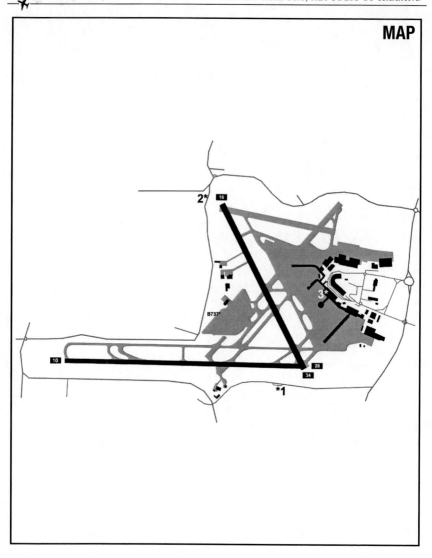

Frequencies

Flight Information Service	118.5
Ground	121.8
Clearance Delivery	121.875
Approach	119.55
Approach	119.925
Approach	121.1
ATIS	124.525

Runways

10/28	8,652ft / 2,637m
11/29	4,393ft / 1,339m
16/34	6,798ft / 2,072m

2. Runway 16

Following the perimeter road around will lead you past the fire station and to the threshold of Runway 16. Parking along the side of the road, you can take good photographs here. This runway is not used as much.

3. Inside Terminal

The Mezzanine Food Court area of the terminal has some views across the aprons and runways which can be useful if the weather's bad. Photography isn't really possible from this spot.

Airlines

Adria Airways
Aer Arann
Air Europa
Aer Lingus
Aer Lingus Regional (Aer Arann)
airBaltic
Air Canada
Air France (CityJet)
Air France Cargo
Air Italy
Air Transat
American Airlines
Arkia Israel Airlines
BH Air
Blue Air
bmi British Midland
bmi Regional
Bulgaria Air
Cimber Sterling
CityJet
Delta Air Lines
DHL Express
Dubrovnik Airline
Emirates
Etihad Airways
Europe Airpost
FedEx Express
FedEx Feeder (Air Contractors)
Flybe

Flybe (Loganair)
Germanwings
Holidays Czech Airlines
Iberia (Air Nostrum)
Jet2
Lufthansa
Luxair
Malev
Monarch
Norwegian Air Shuttle
Onur Air
Orbest Orizonia Airlines
Pegasus Airlines
Ryanair
SATA International
Scandinavian Airlines
Sky Airlines
Spanair
Swiss International Air Lines
S7 Airlines
Tailwind Airlines
Thomson Airways
TNT Airways
Travel Service
Tunisair
Turkish Airlines
United Airlines
UPS Airlines (Star Air)
US Airways

Hotels

Clarion Hotel Dublin Airport

Dublin Airport | +353 (0) 18 08 05 00 | www.clariondublinairport.de

This is the only hotel at Dublin Airport with views of aircraft. This is limited to aircraft landing on Runway 28, and only available from certain rooms. The hotel is a short walk from spotting locations on the perimeter road.

Radisson SAS Great Southern Hotel

Dublin Airport | +353 (0) 18 44 60 00 | www.radissonsas.com

This is a tall hotel set amongst the car parks near the terminal and maintenance area. Some upper rooms may yield views of the aprons and runways. The hotel is fairly expensive.

Nearby Attractions

Casement Aerodrome

Also known as Baldonnel Aerodrome, this is Dublin's GA airport situated a few miles to the south of the city. It has two runways, and is home to the Garda Air Support Unit and its aircraft. You will often find executive aircraft here, also. Spotting is not generally encouraged here, but is possible near the main entrance, underneath the approach path to runway 23.

East Midlands Airport, United Kingdom

EMA | EGNX

Tel: +44 1332 852 852
Web: www.eastmidlandsairport.com
Passengers: 4,113,501 (2010)

Overview

East Midlands deserves a mention in this book as the UK's most notable cargo airport. It successfully transitioned from a quiet regional airport by developing as a hub for cargo airlines such as TNT and UPS. These now serve the airport daily alongside their partners, such as Atlantic Airlines, Star Air and Air Contractors. This is not to belittle the airport as a passenger base, with airlines such as Ryanair, Jet2, Thomas Cook, and Thomson all offering a decent number of services.

Cargo flights operate mostly at night between 2100-0200 from Sunday to Friday. During the daytime you will only likely see a few DHL aircraft parked up, although there are usually more evident on Saturdays. UPS and Star Air aircraft usually park on the eastern cargo ramp, whilst all others use the DHL ramp.

Spotting Locations

1. Crash Gate

Most spotters congregate at the crash gate on the northern side of the airfield as it is an accepted place to spot and offers the best views of all movements. To reach the gate, head to the village of Castle Donington. Close to the Aeropark museum, there's a pub with a small road next to it. This road leads to the crash gate. You can see the passenger terminal and DHL apron, and all runway movements. It is good for photography through holes in the fence and once aircraft are above the fence line. You can also wander along the path which extends along the airport's northern boundary from here.

2. Hangar Area

From the airport's long stay car parks and access roads near DHL, you can drive to an area amongst the hangars which will yield any aircraft receiving maintenance, as well as some executive and light aircraft. You can photograph them through the fence, but don't stay too long in this area.

MAP

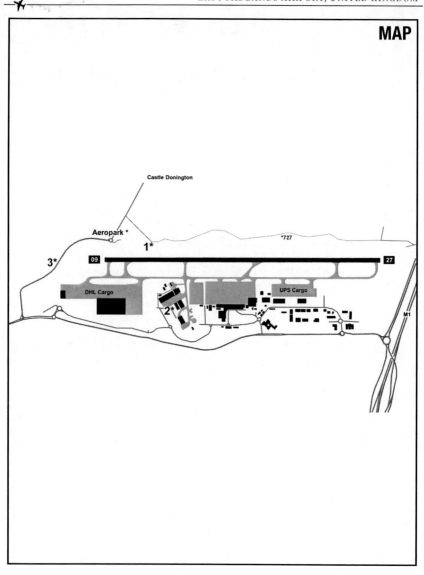

Castle Donington

Aeropark *

1*

3*

09

27

727

DHL Cargo

2*

UPS Cargo

M1

Frequencies
Ground 121.9
ATIS 128.225
Approach 134.175

Runways
09/27 9,491ft / 2,893m

3. Runway End

The road which passes the end of runway 09 (near Donington Race Course) has some areas alongside which are underneath the flight path to the runway. If you're on foot, you can climb a little higher and take photos, or see what is parked on the DHL ramp.

Airlines

Aerologic
Atlantic Airlines
Aurigny Air Services
Austrian Arrows
BH Air
bmi Regional
bmibaby
DHL
DHL (Atlantic Airlines)
DHL (Bluebird Cargo)
DHL (Swiftair)
Eastern Airways
Europe Airpost
Flybe
Icelandair Cargo
Jet2
Jet2 Cargo
Kalitta Air
Loganair
Onur Air
Ryanair
Thomas Cook Airlines
Thomson Airways
Titan Airways
TNT Airways
UPS Airlines
UPS Airlines (Star Air)

Hotels

Radisson Blu East Midlands

Herald Way, Pegasus Business Park, East Midlands Airport DE74 2TU | +44 (0) 1509 670575
www.radissonblu.co.uk/hotel-eastmidlandsairport

A brand new, stylish hotel only a few minutes from the passenger terminal. Its height suggests that movements could be seen from north-facing rooms on the top floor.

Thistle East Midlands Airport

East Midlands Airport, Castle Donington DE74 2SH | +44 845 305 8315 | www.thistle.com

Situated in the car park of the airport, and so very convenient. Unfortunately there are very few rooms that will offer any kind of view, and those that do will be distant of traffic approaching or departing.

Nearby Attractions

East Midlands Aeropark

www.eastmidlandsaeropark.org

The Aeropark is a small outdoor museum situated on the north side of the airport, opposite the DHL cargo apron and very close to the Crash Gate spotting location. The collection includes a variety of British aircraft, including the Vulcan, Nimrod, Viscount and Varsity. It also has a number of helicopters. It also has its own viewing mound which gives you views over the line of the fence alongside the runway.

The park is open Thursday (10.30am-4pm), Saturday (12-5pm), Sunday (10.30am-5pm) between May and September, and Sundays (10.30am-5pm) between October and April. There's a small admission fee.

Coventry Airport

Coventry is home to the Airbase museum and attraction, run by resident Atlantic Airways and their fleet of classic aircraft which they restore on site. The airport is only used for GA and cargo flights at the moment, but has a number of interesting types parked around the field. There's also the Midland Air Museum with a nice collection.

London City Airport, United Kingdom

LCY | EGLC

Tel: +44 207 646 0088
Web: www.londoncityairport.com
Passengers: 2,780,582 (2010)

Overview

London City Airport is a marvel of engineering and inner-city regeneration. It occupies the former Royal Albert Dock in the heart of London, from where it serves the Financial District, whose skyscrapers loom very close to the end of the runway.

The idea was first pitched in 1981, and following feasibility studies, planning consultations, and construction of a 1,080m (3,543ft) runway, it opened for services on 31 May 1987. Later, the runway was extended to allow larger aircraft to land (and reduce the steep angle of approach to 5.5 degrees), and development of new stands and an extended terminal took place.

Today the airport can be busy at times, but is restricted in operations to weekdays, plus Saturday mornings and Sunday afternoons. Traffic is primarily that of BA Cityflyer and other European airlines' commuter fleets linking financial cities, however a number of leisure flights operate at weekends, and of course British Airways' Airbus A318's fly to New York (via Shannon). The airport is also popular with bizjets.

Spotting Locations

1. Opposite Dock

Opposite the airport there is a walkway running the length of the runway with great views. From here you will see every movement, and be able to read off aircraft parked at the terminal. Some parked biz jets are a little awkward to read from here, however. Photography is also great from this spot with a 300mm lens. To get here head for Royal Albert Way, off the A177. The University of East London is here, and there is ample parking space.

2. Runway 27

When heading north on the A177, take a right turn into the industrial estate, and

MAP

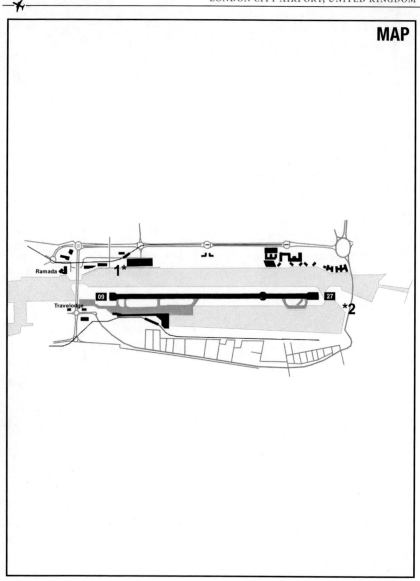

Frequencies

Tower	118.4
Ground	121.825
ATIS	136.35
Approach	132.7

Runway

09/27   4,984ft / 1,508m

then turn left and follow the road under the A177 to a small car park. This spot is very close to the end of Runway 28, so you get a good view down the runway which is perfect for photography.

Airlines

Aer Arann
Alitalia (CityJet)
Blue Islands
British Airways
British Airways (BA CityFlyer)
British Airways (Sun Air)
CityJet
Lufthansa Regional
Luxair
Sky Work Airlines
Swiss European Air Lines

Hotels

London City Airport Travelodge

Hartmann Road, Silvertown, London E16 2BZ | 0871 984 6290 | www.travelodge.co.uk

A short distance from the terminal and on the main access road. Higher rooms facing north have a view over the end of runway 09 and the biz jet ramp. The best ones are 503 to 509. You shouldn't miss too many movements from here. Please note that these are family rooms, so you'll need to request one when booking.

Ramada Hotel and Suites London Docklands

Excel, Royal Victoria Dock, 2 Festoon Way, London E16 1RH | +44 20 7540 4820
www.ramadadocklands.co.uk

This smart and popular business hotel has rooms higher up facing towards the airport, and approach to runway 09. It's a little more distant from the Travelodge, but spotting shouldn't be a problem.

Nearby Attractions

London Heathrow Airport

See separate entry

London Stansted Airport

See separate entry

This page has been intentionally left blank.

London Gatwick Airport, United Kingdom

LGW | EGGK

Tel: +44 844 335 1802
Web: www.gatwickairport.com
Passengers: 31,375,290 (2010)

Overview

Gatwick is London's second largest airport, and situated to the south of the city. It is the London airport where many of the country's charter and low-cost carriers operate, as well as some of the larger airlines from around the world. Due to the recent Open Skies arrangement, a number of the North American airlines relegated to Gatwick have been given access to the more lucrative Heathrow airport, reducing the airport's timetable somewhat.

British Airways retains a healthy presence at Gatwick, operating short, medium and long haul services with a dedicated fleet that will not usually be seen on an average visit to Heathrow.

Gatwick has two terminals – North and South. It is the world's busiest single runway airport. This can lead to lengthy delays and some spectacularly short gaps between departing and arriving traffic.

Sadly Gatwick lost its excellent viewing terrace on the South Terminal in favour of expansion in the early 2000s. This left Gatwick with no official viewing facilities, and it has since proved a very frustrating airport for the enthusiast. Despite being sold to a new owner recently, there are no plans for any official viewing areas.

Spotting Locations

1. Multi-Storey Car Park

The top level of the Multi-Storey car park at the southern end of the South Terminal is a nice spot for logging aircraft on the southern pier, and aircraft on short finals to Runway 26L. Facing into the sun is not ideal, however. Signs at this location indicate that spotters are not welcome to loiter.

2. Runway 08R

Following Charlwood Road and Lowfield Heath Road around the end of Runway

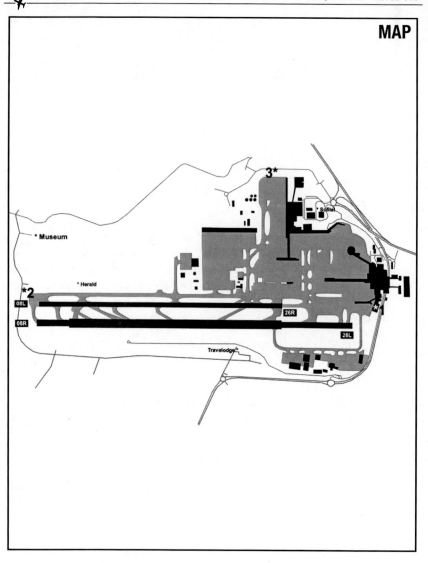

MAP

3*

* Sofitel

* Museum

* Herald

*2

08L

08R

26R

26L

Travelodge *

Frequencies

Tower	134.225
Ground	121.8
Clearance Delivery	121.95
ATIS	136.525
Approach	118.95
Approach	126.825
Approach	129.025

Runways

08L/26R 8,415ft / 2,565m (backup runway)
08R/26L 10,879ft / 3,316m

08R leads to a crash gate which is close to aircraft lining up on the runway. It is possible to photograph or log aircraft, including those on short final to land. This is the most popular spot for spotters these days, however parking is not allowed near the gate itself.

3. Perimeter Road North

The Perimeter Road North runs to the car parks for the North Terminal. It passes the apron where most aircraft using this terminal are parked, and is therefore worth a stop to log what can be seen. Not of use for photography.

Airlines

Adria Airways	Flybe
Aer Lingus	Fly Hellas
Aerosvit Airlines	Hellenic Imperial Airways
Afriqiyah Airways	Hi Fly
AirAsia X	Iceland Express
Air Berlin	Jet2
Air Europa	Korean Air
Air Malta	Lufthansa
Air Moldova	Malev
Air Nigeria	Monarch
Air Transat	Montenegro Airlines
Air Zimbabwe	Norwegian Air Shuttle
airBaltic	Nouvelair
Al-Naser Airlines	Pegasus Airlines
Astraeus Airlines	Rossiya
Aurigny Air Services	Royal Air Maroc
Avianca	Ryanair
Belavia	SATA International
BH Air	Scandinavian Airlines
British Airways	Sky Airlines
Bulgaria Air	Strategic Airlines
Cimber Sterling	Sun Country Airlines
Croatia Airlines	Sunwing Airlines
Cubana	TAP Portugal
Delta Air Lines	Thomas Cook Airlines
easyJet	Thomson Airways
easyJet Switzerland	Titan Airways
Emirates	Tor Air
Estonian Air	Tunisair

Ukraine International Airlines
United Airways
US Airways

Vietnam Airlines
Virgin Atlantic Airways

Hotels

Sofitel London Gatwick Airport

North Terminal, Gatwick Airport RH6 0PH | +44 (0) 12 93 56 70 70 | www.sofitel.com

Smart hotel situated at the North Terminal, and linked via monorail from the South Terminal. Rooms on the higher floors facing the airport have unrivalled views of aircraft movements to both terminals. Expensive.

Travelodge Gatwick Airport

Church Road, Lowfield Heath, Crawley RH11 0PQ | +44 (0) 87 19 84 60 31 | www.travelodge.co.uk

Although its rooms don't offer any realistic views of the airport, it is situated a stone's throw from the southern perimeter, and therefore perfect for the only useful spotting locations. It is a more affordable hotel.

Nearby Attractions

Gatwick Aviation Museum

Lowfield Heath Road, Gatwick, Surrey RH6 0BT | +44 (0) 12 93 86 29 15
www.gatwick-aviation-museum.co.uk

A collection of preserved historic aircraft can be found a mile or so north of the Runway 08R threshold. Mostly military and wartime aircraft. Check the website or call for opening days.

London Heathrow Airport

(see separate entry)

London Heathrow Airport, United Kingdom

LHR | EGGL

Tel: +44 844 335 1801
Web: www.heathrowairport.com
Passengers: 65,881,660 (2010)

Overview

One of the biggest crimes to the spotting community in the United Kingdom of recent years was the removal of the viewing facilities at Heathrow and Gatwick airports. The terraces above the Queen's Building and Terminal 2 at Heathrow were excellent, allowing photography and logging of all movements.

Since the changes, which came about when expansion and terrorist threats became priority, spotters have had to find alternatives around the airport. All is not lost, however, as photography and logging is still possible at arguably one of the best airports in Europe for movements.

Heathrow airport is Europe's busiest and at times is very overcrowded. The variety of airlines operating here is mouth-watering to the enthusiast, and come from all corners of the globe. It is the operating and maintenance base for both British Airways and Virgin Atlantic. The recently Open Skies agreement has also attracted a number of new carriers to the airport which were previously relegated to Gatwick and other airports.

Heathrow has two parallel runways, 09L/27R and 09R/27L. Patterns of runway assignment between landing and departing usually switch during the day. In the central area is terminals 1 and 3, with a new Terminal 2 under construction. Terminal 5, for British Airways flights, is to the west, whilst Terminal 4 is located to the south east of the runways. Cargo aircraft park to the south, and maintenance areas are to the east.

Spotting Locations

1. Myrtle Avenue

This is one of the most popular spots at Heathrow, but is only useful when aircraft are landing on runway 27L. The spot gets its name from a small residential street close to Hatton Cross, with a grass area at the end. Spotters congregate on this area to log and photograph aircraft as they pass low overhead. There is very limited parking, so it's best to walk from Hatton Cross Tube Station.

MAP

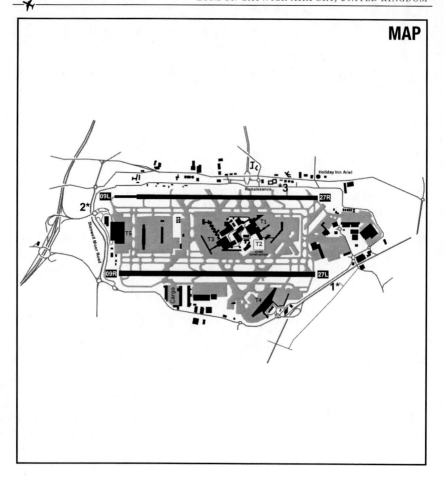

Frequencies

Tower	118.7
Tower	124.475
Ground	121.7
Ground	121.9
Clearance Delivery	121.975
ATIS	113.75
ATIS	115.1
ATIS	121.85
ATIS	128.075
Approach	119.725
Approach	120.4
Approach	127.525
Approach	134.975

Runways

09L/27R	12,799ft / 3,901m
09R/27L	12,008ft / 3,660m

2. Runway 09L Approach

Stanwell Moor Road runs the length of the western perimeter of the airport, behind Terminal 5. At its northern end there is often space to park up at the side of the road. Aircraft pass low overhead on approach to runway 09L, and are also visible approaching 09R (but it's hard to photograph those).

3. Academy/Renaissance Hotel

Even if you're not staying in the Renaissance Hotel, the car park next to it was formerly the home of the Heathrow Visitors Centre. Today it is the Heathrow Academy and has an enthusiast's shop. From here you can get good views of all movements, and photographs of aircraft on the northern runway (09L/27R). This spot is located off the Northern Perimeter Road.

Airlines

Aegean Airlines	British Airways	Japan Airlines
Aer Lingus	British Airways	Jat Airways
Aeroflot	World Cargo	Jet Airways
Air Algerie	Brussels Airlines	Kenya Airways
Air Astana	Bulgaria Air	Kingfisher Airlines
Air Canada	Cathay Pacific	KLM
Air China	Cathay Pacific Cargo	KLM CityHopper
Air France	China Airlines	Korean Air
Air India	China Eastern Airlines	Korean Air Cargo
Air Malta	Croatia Airlines	Kuwait Airways
Air Mauritius	Cyprus Airways	Libyan Arab Airlines
Air New Zealand	Delta Air Lines	LOT Polish Airlines
Air Transat	DHL	Lufthansa
Alitalia	EgyptAir	Lufthansa Regional
Alitalia (Air One)	El Al	(Contact Air)
All Nippon Airways	Emirates	Lufthansa Regional
American Airlines	Ethiopian Airlines	(Eurowings)
Arik Air	Etihad Airways	Malaysia Airlines
Asiana Airlines	Etihad Crystal Cargo	MASKargo
Austrian Airlines	EVA Air	Oman Air
Austrian Arrows	EVA Air Cargo	Pakistan International
Azerbaijan Airline	FedEx Express	Airlines
Biman Bangladesh	Finnair	Qantas
Airlines	Gulf Air	Qatar Airways
Blue1	Iberia	Royal Air Maroc
bmi British Midland	Icelandair	Royal Air Maroc Cargo
bmi Regional	Iran Air	Royal Brunei Airlines

Royal Jordanian
Royal Jordanian Cargo
Saudi Arabian Airlines
Scandinavian Airlines
Singapore Airlines
Singapore Airlines Cargo
South African Airways
SriLankan Airlines

Swiss International
Air Lines
Syrian Air
TAM Airlines
TAP Portugal
TAROM
Thai Airways International
Transaero

Tunisair
Turkish Airlines
Turkmenistan Airlines
United Airlines
US Airways
Uzbekistan Airlines
Virgin Atlantic Airways
Vueling

Hotels

Renaissance London Heathrow

140 Bath Road, Hounslow TW6 2AQ | +44 (0) 20 88 97 63 63 | www.marriott.com

This is one of the best spotting hotels in the world, if you request a room overlooking the airport. All movements on the northern runway can be read off and photographed easily. Movements around the terminals are easy to spot. Those using SBS can continue to spot throughout the night. Although this hotel is not the cheapest at Heathrow, the quality of spotting makes up for it and it offers special spotter packages through its website.

Holiday Inn London Heathrow Ariel

118 Bath Road, Harlington, Hayes UB3 5AJ | +44 (0) 20 89 90 00 00 | www.holidayinn.com

Another good spotting hotel at Heathrow. Even-numbered rooms between 270 and 284 have the best views of aircraft using the northern runway and terminal areas. Photography is possible. The hotel is more affordable than the Renaissance.

Nearby Attractions

Brooklands Museum

Weybridge, Surrey KT13 0QN | +44 (0) 19 32 85 54 65 | www.brooklandsmuseum.com

The former racing circuit and airfield was the production site for most Vickers aircraft for many years. Today the site is largely used by Mercedes-Benz for testing, however a museum in one corner has an excellent collection of historic buildings and aircraft built at the site. These include Vickers Viscount, VC-10s, Varsity, Vanguard, a Concorde prototype and many more. The museum also covers the famous racing circuit.

London City Airport

(see separate entry)

London Gatwick Airport

(see separate entry)

London Luton Airport

(see separate entry)

London Luton Airport, United Kingdom

LTN | EGLC
Web: www.london-luton.co.uk
Passengers: 8,738,717 (2010)

Overview

Luton is London's fourth largest airport, and is situated some 30 miles north on the main M1 motorway linking the capital with the north of the country. It opened in 1938 and served as an air base in the Second World War.

Today the airport is a busy gateway for low cost carriers and holiday charter airlines. It is the home base of easyJet, Thomson Airways and Monarch Airlines. Ryanair and Wizz Air also have a decent presence at the airport. A small number of cargo airliners also pass through each day.

Luton is perhaps best known amongst enthusiasts for the large variety of business jets which pass through on a regular basis. The airport has many ramps and hangars dedicated to this traffic, and it is said you've had a bad day if you count less than 40 on any visit.

Luton has quite a cramped and confusing central area which includes the terminals, car parks, roads, hotels and administration buildings. You will see signs around this area discouraging spotters from stopping. It is possible to do a quick stop and log in order to catch some aircraft not visible from anywhere else. If you have some time to spend here, it's best to spend it at the area alongside the runway, which is well away from hassle.

Spotting Locations

1. Terminal Building & Car Park

Inside the passenger terminal there are limited views of the main apron and taxiway without actually going airside. The Short Stay Car Park alongside the terminal is also a good place to log some of the aircraft parked at the gates and remote stands.

2. Central Area

Driving around the access roads to the hangars, cargo centre and other parts of

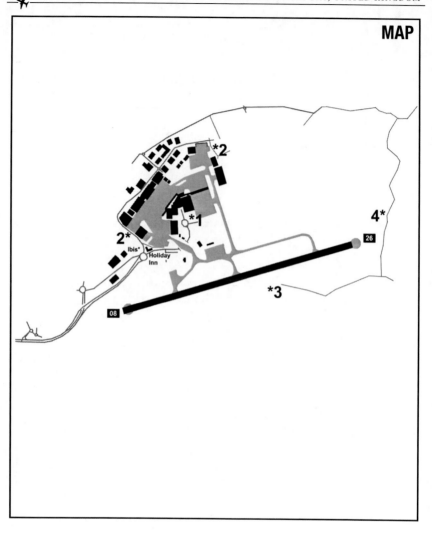

MAP

*2

*1

4*

2*

Ibis*

Holiday
Inn

26

*3

08

Frequencies

Tower	132.55
Ground	121.75
ATIS	120.575
Approach	128.75
Approach	129.55

Runway
08/26   7,087ft / 2,160m

the central complex will offer glimpses of many business jets and other aircraft parked around the various aprons. Signs discourage spotters from parking in these areas, so make only quick stops to log what you can see. You can park at the Holiday Inn for a small fee.

3. Crash Gate

Head away from the terminal area towards the M1. Turn right at the second roundabout and then right again towards Wheathamstead. After a couple of miles, turn left at a crossroads, under a railway bridge and up the hill. Turn left at the next junction and keep right. Turn left at the houses, and park alongside the road when it reaches the fence. Keep the crash gate clear at all times! Views of aircraft using the runway are good from here, and photography is possible.

4. Runway 26

Follow directions for the Crash Gate spot (above), but turn right at the houses. Then take the first left. The road will pass very close to the end of Runway 26. Excellent photographs of aircraft on short finals can be taken here, although parking is a problem.

Airlines

Aer Arann
Atlantic Airlines
Blue Air
British Airways World Cargo (DHL Express)
DHL Express
easyJet
El Al
Flybe
Israir
MNG Airlines
Monarch
Ryanair
Thomson Airways
VarigLog
Wizz Air

Hotels

Holiday Inn Express Luton Airport

2 Percival Way, Luton LU2 9GP | +44 (0) 1582 58 91 00 | www.hiexpress.com

Rooms facing the airport are all great for logging aircraft, and also have plenty of opportunities for good photographs. The hotel is relatively cheap.

Ibis Hotel

Osborne Road, Luton LU1 3HJ | +44 (0) 8701 97 71 66 | www.premierinn.com

A comfortable and affordable travel inn located under the approach to Runway 08. Aircraft viewing opportunities will be very minimal, but the central terminal area is very close to the hotel.

Nearby Attractions

London Heathrow Airport

See separate entry

London Stansted Airport

See separate entry

London Stansted Airport, United Kingdom

STN | EGSS

Tel: +44 844 335 1803
Web: www.stanstedairport.com
Passengers: 18,573,803 (2010)

Overview

Stansted is a fairly busy airport 30 miles north east of London saw dramatic growth in the mid-1990s when the impressive single terminal building, designed by Sir Norman Foster, was opened to replace the inadequate facilities on the original site.

The airport had started life as a bomber base and maintenance depot in the Second World War. The potential for passenger operations was realised when the British Airports Authority (BAA) took over in 1966.

When low-cost airlines Ryanair, Go and Buzz wanted cheaper access to London, Stansted was chosen and it quickly grew to handle the demand. Go was quickly swallowed by easyJet, and Buzz by Ryanair, leaving these two airlines as the main operators. Today a number of other low-cost airlines also have a large presence at Stansted, including Air Berlin. A number of charter, long-haul and cargo airlines can also be found operating through Stansted on a daily basis.

Stansted has a single runway, though there have been plans around to build another, once planning permission is approved and the locals appeased, for a number of years.

Sadly no official viewing locations were ever provided, and watching the action can be difficult if you're not catching a flight. On the old airport site across the runway, biz jets are handled and maintained, and a resident L1011 Tristar is used as a trainer.

Spotting Locations

1. Old Terminal Area

On the opposite side of the airport close to the Runway 05 end is the old terminal area, now used for maintenance, executive jets, and aircraft storage. There is a long-term resident L1011 Tristar here, and on any day there are likely to be some exotic business jets present. From the airport exit from the M11, take the

MAP

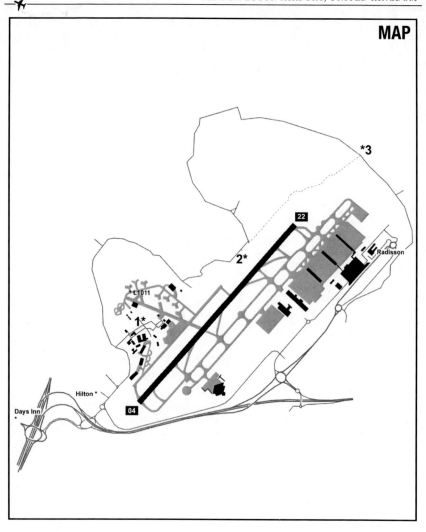

Frequencies

Tower 125.55
Ground 121.725
Director 126.95
Clearance Delivery 121.95
ATIS 127.175
Approach 120.625

Runway
04/22   10,003ft / 3,049m

2nd exit at the roundabout instead of heading to the Terminal. This leads to the Long Stay Car Parks. Bypass these and follow Round Coppice Road, turning into Bury Lodge Lane. After passing the village of Burton End, look out for places to pull up on the right and log what you can see. This may take some perseverance. Security has been known to move people on from this area.

2. Opposite Runway

Following on from the first location, turn down Bury Lodge Lane, then Belmer Road. Soon, you will find a straight stretch of road where most days there are plenty of cars parked at the side of the road. Walk through any of the gaps in the trees and you'll find a grass area overlooking the runway and parts of the passenger terminal and cargo ramps. You will see all movements from here, and photography is possible.

2. Runway 23

At the end of Runway 23 is a field from which aircraft on short final can be photographed and logged. It is of no use for watching ground movements as a hill is in the way. To reach this spot, take the road past the terminal, but continue to Molehill Green and Elsenham. Go past Molehill Green and take a left at a technology factor along Green Street. Park your car at the end and walk into the field.

Airlines

Air Berlin
Albanian Airlines
Asiana Cargo
Atlantic Airways
Aurigny Air Services
British Airways (BA CityFlyer)
British Airways World Cargo
BH Air
Belle Air
Belle Air Europe
bmibaby
easyJet
FedEx Express
FedEx Express (Air Contractors)
FedEx Express (Swiftair)

Fly Hellas
Germanwings
Jet2 Cargo
Monarch Airlines
Onur Air
Pegasus Airlines
Pegasus Airlines (IZair)
Royal Jordanian Cargo
Ryanair
Thomas Cook Airlines
Thomson Airways
Titan Airways
TNT Airways
Turkish Airlines (Anadolujet)
UPS Airlines

Hotels

Radisson SAS Stansted Airport

Waltham Close, Stansted Airport, Essex CM24 1PP | +44 (0) 12 79 66 10 12
www.stansted.radissonsas.com

A very smart, modern hotel at Stansted with prices at the higher end. Some higher rooms facing the airport have views over the Ryanair pier and Runway 23 threshold. The hotel is only a few metres from the Terminal.

Hilton London Stansted

Round Coppice Road, London Stansted, Essex CM24 1SF | +44 (0) 12 79 68 08 00 | www.hilton.com

At the opposite end of the airport, close to the M11 and Long Stay Car Parks. The Hilton is another pricey hotel at Stansted. Some rooms facing the airport have views of aircraft on short final to Runway 05, and on the taxiway linking it.

Days Inn

Welcome Break Service Area J8, M11, Birchanger Green, Bishops Stortford CM23 5QZ
+44 (0) 12 79 65 64 77 | www.daysinn.com

A much more affordable option is the Days Inn located off the M11 at the entrance to Stansted Airport in the service station. No views of movements are available here, but the hotel is a very short distance from the airport.

Nearby Attractions

Imperial War Museum Duxford

Duxford, Cambridgeshire CB22 4QR | +44 (0) 12 23 83 72 67 | duxford.iwm.org.uk

Possibly Europe's finest aviation museum. IWM Duxford is a former air base which served in both World Wars. Its collections cover the earliest times of flight, through the history of military and commercial aircraft. Of particular note to the enthusiast may be the preserved Concorde, Vickers VC-10 and Viscount, Trident, Bristol Britannia and De Havilland Comet. Open daily (except 24-26 December) from 10am to 6pm (4pm from late October to mid-March). Adults £16.50, Concessions £13.20, Children (0-15) free.

Manchester Airport, United Kingdom

LGW | EGLC

Tel: +44 871 271 0711
Web: www.manchesterairport.co.uk
Passengers: 17,759,015 (2010)

Overview

Manchester has become one of the favourite airports in the UK for enthusiasts thanks to its excellent viewing facilities and fairly varied mix of movements, which can be pleasingly busy at certain times of the day.

Manchester is one of the UK's most important airports and has long been popular with both a charter and scheduled carriers. The north of England gateway has long retained its position as the third busiest in the country, after Heathrow and Gatwick in the London area. In recent years, coupled with periods of significant expansion, a number of low cost airlines have started services here.

Manchester Airport has three passenger terminals and a cargo terminal, along with an extensive maintenance area comprising large hangars and bays. The airport has two parallel runways.

Whilst long haul flights were slow to establish at Manchester, today the airport enjoys a number of links across the Atlantic with American Airlines, Delta, PIA, United and US Airways all plying their trade on a daily basis. In the opposite direction, Emirates offer three daily flights to Dubai (including one using their Airbus A380), Qatar Airways and Singapore Airlines provide popular links with Asia and the Middle East. A number of cargo carriers provide daily widebody aircraft for added spice.

Spotting Locations

1. Runway Visitor Park

What must be the best official viewing facility in the UK is located at Manchester. The Runway Visitor Park was built on the north side of Runway 06L/24R to replace facilities lost when the new runway was built and terminals extended. Purpose-built mounds raise the enthusiast over the height of the fence to allow photography of aircraft on the runway and taxiway. Also at the AVP is a hobby shop, café, toilets and various preserved airliners – some of which are open to

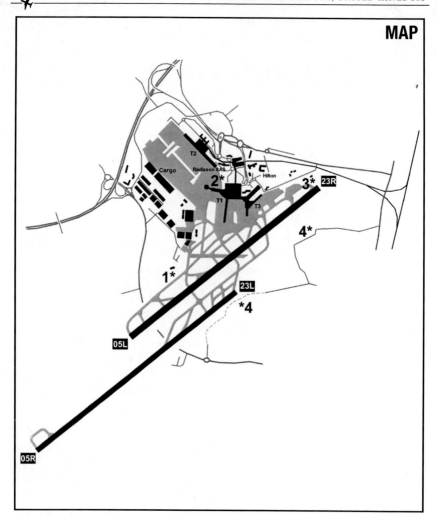

Frequencies

Tower	119.4
Ground	121.7
Ground	121.85
Ground	125.375
Clearance Delivery	121.7
ATIS	121.975
ATIS	128.175
Approach	118.575
Approach	121.35
Approach	135.0

Runways
05L/23R 10,000ft / 3,048m
05R/23L 10,007ft / 3,050m

the public. These include a DC-10 section, Concorde (inside its own 'hangar'), Trident, Nimrod and Avro RJX. The park is open daily (except 25/26 December) from 8am till dusk. There is an entrance fee depending on how long you stay.

2. Multi-Storey Car Park

For many years the top level of the Short Stay Car Park outside Terminal 1 was also the spotter's choice. It offered fantastic views over the cargo and maintenance ramps, as well as Terminal 2, parts of Terminal 1, and the runways in the distance. Cafe and hobby shop facilities were also located here. However, in 2006 the area was cleared and the shop relocated to the arrivals hall of Terminal 1. Spotting and photography are still good from the car park's open roof. This is a good spot to log what's not visible from the Runway Visitor Park.

3. Airport Hotel Pub

Located at the threshold of Runway 24R. The beer garden here backs up to the taxiway and holding point for the runway and is ideal for landing shots. A very pleasant summer afternoon can be held here, with food and refreshments on tap.

4. South Side

Along the southern boundary of the airport, a number of unofficial spots can be reached by car which offer great opportunities to take photographs of aircraft on the runways, and views across most of the terminal areas. From the Airport Hotel, take a right and the third exit at the roundabout. At the lights, turn right again onto Moss Lane. Half a mile further on, you will find an area suitable for parking (being careful not to obstruct the gate) with the airport in front of you.

Airlines

Adria Airways	Astraeus Airlines	Cathay Pacific Cargo
Aer Arann	Aurigny Air Services	China Airlines Cargo
Aer Lingus	Austrian Airlines	City Airline
Aer Lingus Regional	BH Air	CityJet
(Aer Arann)	Belavia	Croatia Airlines
Air Berlin	bmi British Midland	Cyprus Airways
Air France	bmi Regional	Delta Air Lines
Air France (Regional)	bmibaby	Dubrovnik Airline
Air France (CityJet)	British Airways	easyJet
Air Malta	British Airways	easyJet Switzerland
Air Transat	(BA CityFlyer)	Emirates
Airblue	British Airways (Sun Air)	Etihad Airways
American Airlines	Brussels Airlines	FedEx Express (Air
AtlasJet	Cargolux	Contractors)

Finnair	Neos	Air Lines
Flybe	Norwegian Air Shuttle	TAP Portugal
Fly Hellas	Onur Air	Thomas Cook Airlines
Germanwings	Orbest Orizonia Airlines	Thomas Cook Airlines
Great Wall Airlines	Pakistan International	Scandinavia
Holidays Czech Airlines	Airlines	Thomson Airways
Iberia (Air Nostrum)	Pegasus Airlines	Titan Airways
Icelandair	Qatar Airways	Tor Air
Jet2	Ryanair	Turkish Airlines
KLM	SATA International	Tunisair
KLM CityHopper	Scandinavian Airlines	United Airlines
Lufthansa	Singapore Airlines	US Airways
Lufthansa Cargo	Star Air	Virgin Atlantic Airways
Lufthansa Regional	Strategic Airlines	VLM (CityJet)
(Eurowings)	Swiss European Air Lines	
Monarch	Swiss International	

Hotels

Radisson SAS Hotel

Chicago Avenue, Manchester M90 3RA | +44 (0) 161 490 5000 | www.radissonsas.com

The best hotel for spotting at Manchester. Located behind Terminal 2, rooms on high floors overlook the aprons and the runways in the distance. The restaurant also offers this view. Some good opportunities for photographs with a long lens. The hotel is rarely cheap.

Hilton Manchester Airport

Outwood Lane, Manchester M90 4WP | +44 (0) 161 435 3040 | www.hilton.com

Located close to the terminals, though with very few views of aircraft movements. Rooms can be reasonably priced. The terminals are a very short walk from this hotel.

Nearby Attractions

Manchester Museum of Science and Industry

Liverpool Road, Castlefield, Manchester M3 4FP | +44 (0) 161 832 2244 | www.mosi.org.uk

Located in the heart of Manchester, this museum has a whole building dedicated to aircraft. Collection includes a Dragon Rapide, Avro 504, Bristol Belvedere, Bristol Sycamore, Trident 3B cockpit and many more. Museum is open daily 10am-5pm except 24-26 December and 1 January. Free entry.